8536500000258

# FIRE ATTACK

## The Strategy and Tactics
## of
## Initial Company Response

D1706878

Firefighting is not an exact science and it involves many hazardous, unknown variables. *Fire Attack* is not intended to provide all the training necessary for safe fireground operations. OnGUARD shall not be responsible for any misunderstanding or misapplication of the information presented in this program. In addition, OnGUARD shall not be liable for any death or injury resulting from the application of information presented in this course.

## ONGUARD
### TRAINING FOR LIFE

© 1987 OnGUARD, Inc.
A Division of Emergency Resource, Inc.
Fort Collins, Colorado

628.92

ISBN 1-56916-001-5
Printed in the United States of America

Eighth Printing, November 1996

# ACKNOWLEDGEMENTS

Randy R. Bruegman

OnGUARD would like to acknowledge Randy R. Bruegman, Executive Producer and contributing author for the *Fire Attack* series. Mr. Bruegman is the Fire Chief for the Hoffman Estates, Illinois Fire Department. He has over 20 years of experience as both a paid and a volunteer firefighter. Chief Bruegman holds a Master of Science degree in Management, a Bachelor's degree in Business Administration, and an Associate of Arts degree in Fire Science. He is the Vice Chairman of the International Association of Fire Chiefs Accreditation Committee and serves on the Editorial Advisory Board for *Fire Chief Magazine*.

# MODULE ONE

## UNDERSTANDING FIRE ATTACK

# VIDEO NOTES

_____

_____

_____

_____

_____

_____

_____

_____

_____

_____

_____

_____

_____

_____

_____

_____

_____

_____

_____

_____

_____

_____

_____

_____

_____

# FIRE BEHAVIOR

One way to help understand the importance of fire behavior is to consider the divorce rate in this country. If you are married or have a "significant other" in your life, you can identify with the need for partners to understand each other if the relationship is to survive. A lack of understanding most often leads to the destruction of that relationship. A parallel can be drawn to an officer's understanding of fire behavior. The better the understanding, the better the officer will be able to deal with the problems the fire presents. A lack of understanding on the officer's part can lead to the destruction of a structure and/or loss of life. To be an effective fire fighter, company officer, or incident commander understanding your fire problem and its behavior will give you the advantage during fireground operations.

SO, LET'S GET IN AND STUDY FIRE BEHAVIOR!

## Fire Behavior Factors

An important part of an officer's size-up will be the ability to make an accurate fire behavior prediction. Understanding fire behavior factors will greatly assist the officer in determining what is happening and what is likely to happen. These factors will have an impact on safety, strategy, and the use of resources. These factors are:

1. Heat Release
2. Heat Transfer
3. Flashover
4. Backdraft
5. Ignition Temperature
6. Fire Load
7. Heat and Smoke Travel
8. Fire gases
9. Thermal Stratification
10. Weather Conditions

## 1. Heat

Heat is described in several ways, all of which bear a definite relationship to each other. The following definitions help to better understand the concept of heat, the following definitions are necessary:

***British Thermal Unit (BTU).*** *One BTU is defined as the amount of heat required to raise the temperature of 1 pound of water 1 degree Fahrenheit (when the measurement is performed at 60 degrees F).*

***Calorie.*** *One calorie is the amount of heat required to raise the temperature of 1 gram of water 1 degree Centigrade.*

The equivalency between a BTU and a calorie is that

**1 BTU = 252 calories**

Knowledge of the types of materials present in a given fire situation and their heat values is important and can assist you in determining the amount of water to apply and the behavior of other materials within the environment.

***Heat of Combustion:*** One other term is important in under standing the concept of heat. *This is heat of combustion or the amount of heat that will be released by a substance when it is completely consumed by fire.*

There are a number of variables that influence the output of heat from burning materials. Some of these factors are:

1. The amount or area of solid combustibles exposed to heat and oxygen.

2. The area of free surface of the liquid (in case of flammable substances, to give off vapor pressure).

3. The conductivity of solids (woods, etc.), which can influence the amount of heat given off when materials burn.

Even though the heat values (in BTUs) of various materials are not precise, they provide us with necessary information for developing the concepts of "fireloading" and heat absorption qualities of water. *Fire load encompasses the total number of British Thermal Units that might be produced during a fire in a building or given area.* Some examples of the heat of combustion values of various materials are shown in the following table.

| Materials | BTU/lb. |
|---|---|
| Asphalt | 17,150 |
| Cotton Batting | 7,000 |
| Gasoline | 19,250 |
| Paper | 7,900 |
| Polystyrene | 18,000 |
| Polyvinyl Chloride | 7,500 to 9,500 |
| Wood | 7,500 to 9,500 |

**Effects on Tactics:** The following factors affect fire fighter safety as well as add to exposure problems, and significantly impact the amount of resources needed:
   * The amount of heat being released
   * Length of time crews can operate before relief is needed
   * The amount of water needed for control.

In addition to the heat value of materials, fire fighting operations must concern themselves with the transfer of heat from place to place.

## 2. Heat Transfer

There are three basic methods by which heat from the combustion of materials is transferred:
   * conduction
   * convection
   * radiation.

Let us examine each one of these separately.

*Conduction: Conduction is the transfer of heat from one material to another, from molecule to molecule, of substances that are in contact with each other.* The heat is transmitted by molecular activity that causes excess vibrations in the hotter portion of a substance. This, in turn, will promote activity in the cooler portions with a resulting rise in heat. Heat flows from a hotter object to a cooler object. It is important to remember that some materials are better conductors than others. Conduction of heat can take place in a fire building through walls and floors via pipes and metal structural elements, as seen in the following diagram.

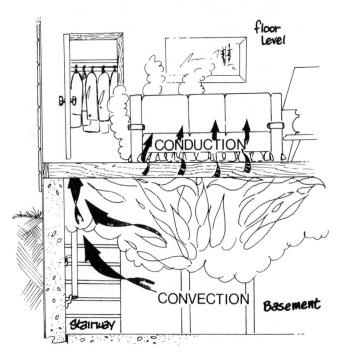

*Convection: Convection is the transfer of heat from one point to another by means of a circulating liquid or gas.* Convective heat transfer is perhaps the most important and most frequently observed mechanism of heat transfer in the spread of fires involving combustible materials.

The combustion of ordinary materials produces gases that are lighter than air, and these gases will rise to upper areas of the room and throughout the building involved.

At higher levels, the heated volume of gas may give up some of its heat, transfer it, and thus progressively raise the temperature in the area. Simply stated, <u>hot gases, vapors, and liquids rise by convection to transfer heat.</u> A hot air heating system is an example of convection, whereby cold air is drawn into the plenum chamber, heated, and circulated

6

through ducts. The air cools and returns from a complete cycle of convection currents.

*Radiation:* *Radiation is the transfer of heat from one material to another in the absence of matter.* Heat energy occurs in exactly the same form as light; that is, in the form of rays of heat. These rays travel through space as units of electro-magnetic energy. Radiation energy travels in straight lines, and it will pass through any visibly transparent medium such as air, glass, water, and transparent plastics with only a small absorption of energy that will slightly heat the transparent substance. Likewise, heat rays may be reflected off of materials.

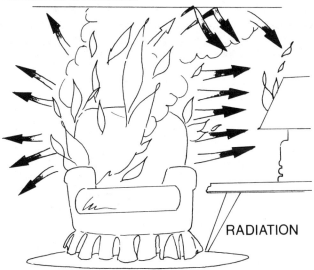

RADIATION

The color and degree of opacity of a substance are factors which influence how heat rays will be absorbed. Black or dark-colored materials readily absorb heat rays. Heat exposure of combustible materials by radiation is a danger during fires in which flames of a large volume are produced, and where radiation from combustible substances falls on nearby materials that can become heated to the point of ignition. Cooling of radiation-heated materials must be initiated quickly in such instances. The water does not act to halt the heat radiation received at the surface; rather the surface heat is transferred by conduction to the water and is cooled by this action.

In fire situations, all three methods of heat transfer will be encountered.

**Direct Flame:** Direct flame impingement on materials will have a pronounced effect. Depending on

the material, the flame and resulting fire propagation may completely consume the material or may only char or blacken the exterior surfaces of the material. Other factors affecting direct flame impingement and its results are:

1. Ignition temperature
2. Flashpoint
3. Rate of combustion
4. Caloric value (amount of heat to be liberated)
5. Texture of material
6. Air currents (or lack of)

Direct flame impingement on fabrics used for fire fighter protective clothing is important. Is the fabric inherently fire-resistive (wool, or other densely woven fabric)? Is the fabric fire-resistive by specific process or design?

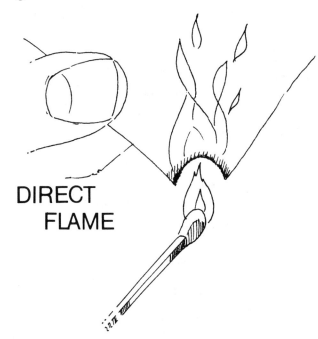

DIRECT FLAME

**Effects on Tactics:** Failure of an officer to recognize or anticipate the effects of heat transfer can result in fire fighting efforts being directed toward one area of a structure, when the real problem is occurring or spreading in another area.

In addition to spreading to other portions of the structure, this spread of heat can endanger the safety

of occupants, hamper rescue efforts, drastically increase the amount of damage, increase the risk of spread to exposures, and endanger the safety of fire fighters. The officer should be aware of how heat transfer can affect body temperature and how long and how safely fire fighters can function.

## 3. & 4. Flashover and Backdraft

On a daily basis fire fighters experience two common conditions inherent to structure fires--backdraft and flashover. Unfortunately, these two common conditions are frequently classified as similar or defined together for simplicity. They are diametrically different, however, in regard to their physical and chemical composition. The results of these conditions are often similar, yielding increased property damage, and/or injury and death to fire fighters.

Are you familiar with potential backdraft or flashover conditions and their warning signs? If you recognize the warning signs, you can adjust your fire fighting operations and techniques accordingly. Let's look at these two conditions and examine their characteristic elements.

*Flashover: A very basic definition of flashover is the ignition of combustibles in an area heated by convection and radiation, or a combination of the two.* The combustible substances in a room are heated to their ignition points, and almost simultaneously combustion of the materials occur. Eventually, the entire area is preheated to its ignition temperature and becomes fully involved in fire in a matter of seconds.

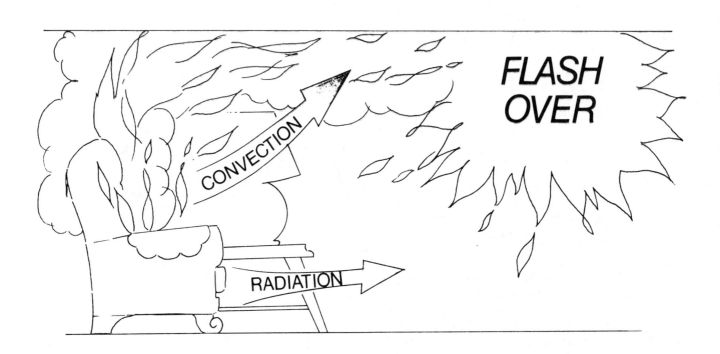

**Warning Signs.** Some of the warning signs of imminent flashover are intense heat, free-burning fire, unburned articles starting to smoke, and fog streams turning to steam a short distance from the nozzle. To reduce the chance of flash over, temperatures need to be lowered quickly by water application, ventilation, or a combination of both. Remember, flashover is a leading cause of injury and death to firefighters across the country. Appropriate hose line size, ventilation, and proper attack methods by first due companies will reduce the risk to fire personnel.

8

**Backdraft:** *The introduction of oxygen to a confined-space that is pressurized with heated flammable gases deficient in oxygen, resulting in an explosive force.* As a fire develops, the combustion process creates an atmosphere that is deficient in oxygen and can lead to the possibility of a backdraft occurring. This is also referred to as a smoke explosion. <u>The difference between a flashover and backdraft is the amount of oxygen present. In a flashover, there is adequate oxygen available for combustion, and the fire is free-burning prior to the flashover. In a backdraft, there is insufficient oxygen for active burning, and the fire is smoldering in an oxygen-deficient atmosphere.</u>

Normally, sufficient oxygen is present during most fires so that the conditions leading to a backdraft are minimized. However, when oxygen is depleted and the fire begins to smolder, an oxygen-deficient atmosphere is created in the fire area. When conditions like this develop, gases such as carbon monoxide and carbonaceous particle smoke or suspensions are produced. These are capable of reacting with oxygen.

This creates a threat of explosion if oxygen is improperly allowed to enter the structure. The accumulated gases will ignite readily, spreading fire or causing a violent explosion. Due to temperatures in the room, the fuel is creating ignitable vapors at or above their ignition temperatures. All that is needed is oxygen in order to complete the fire triangle.

**Signs Indicating Potential Backdraft:**

1. Seriously evaluate fires where the smoke is restricted or confined by a structure.
2. Smoke will be issuing, under pressure, from any available opening. Don't let minimal natural ventilation trick you.
3. Doors and windows may be hot to the touch. In addition, windows may appear to be dark. This darkness is heavy concentrations of thick smoke behind the glass!
4. Expect heavy, dense smoke. In addition, the smoke may appear to be turbulent or boiling because it is under pressure; the smoke is escaping, and it is expanding as it escapes.
5. When doors or windows are opened into the fire building, air is drawn in.

Backdraft

9

**Effects on Tactics:** When backdraft conditions are present, the officer must understand the consequences if entry is attempted prior to ventilation. If oxygen is introduced before the inside pressure is relieved, the resultant explosion can blow fire fighters and their hoses to that great fire station in the sky. Ventilation is the first priority and must be closely coordinated with attack efforts.

Officers should also be aware that the potential for back draft exists in buildings, rooms, attics, or any other confined space.

<u>Ventilation above a fire must precede entry into the structure so the heat, smoke, and fire gases will be reduced along with the potential for backdraft.</u> The success of this operation is dependent upon:

1. <u>Recognition</u> by first-in companies of a potential backdraft
2. <u>Communication</u> between fire attack and ventilation teams
3. <u>Timing</u> between fire attack and ventilation teams, which results in ventilation preceding entry into the structure

## 5. Ignition Temperature

*The physical properties of a material are those properties that change when acted upon by external forces of energy (such as the heat energy of a fire).*

When no change in the composition of the material occurs, the material does not combine with its surroundings.

Solid materials such as wood, paper products, fabrics of all kinds, and plastics become complicated compounds of hydrogen and carbon, with other elements such as oxygen, sulfur, nitrogen, etc. These materials must undergo a chemical decomposition called pyrolysis from heat before ignition can occur. This also applies to certain combustible liquids.

All combustible materials do not catch fire or begin to burn at the same point or at any minimum temperature. The point at which they ignite is unique to each substance and is determined by the composition and properties of that particular material. In order for the chemical reaction we call "burning" to take place, the molecules of a combustible material must be brought up to a certain temperature by the addition of heat energy so that the substance's molecules are ready to combine with the oxygen molecules in the air.

This temperature is referred to as the ignition temperature. ***Ignition temperature*** *(self-ignition or auto-ignition) is the minimum temperature to which a substance must be heated in air to ignite independently of the heated or heating element.* At this temperature, the combustion reaction continues without any external input of heat, since the substance gives off heat by its own combustion and the burning becomes self-sustaining.

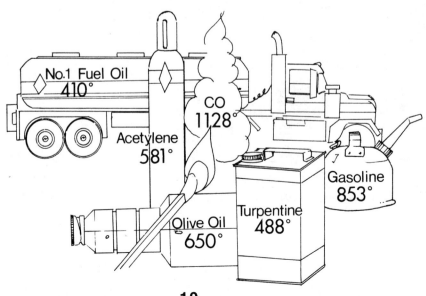

**10**

Remember, although a substance may burn at a certain temperature in a particular fire situation, if the situation is changed even slightly, the ignition temperature will also change. In actual fire situations, the conditions surround ing combustible materials may vary in many ways. For this reason, ignition temperatures of materials are approximations and should be viewed in that context. However, they provide us with some data from which we can make certain value judgments in the field.

| Ignition Materials | Temperature (F) |
|---|---|
| Asphalt | 950 |
| Cotton Batting | 450 |
| Gasoline | 500 to 850 |
| Paper | 450 |
| Polystyrene | 900 to 950 |
| Polyvinyl Chloride | 800 to 900 |
| Wood (sawdust) | 400 to 500 |
| Wood (fir, oak, pine) | 450 to 500 |

## 6. Fire Loads

When a fire develops and begins to spread throughout a structure, every pound of combustible material within the building has the potential of increasing the severity of the fire. Knowledge of the kind and amount of combustibles likely to be present in any given occupancy is extremely important for making a realistic evaluation of the total fire hazard. This can be accomplished by calculating the fire load prior to an incident.

*Fire load* encompasses the total number of BTUs that might evolve during a fire in the building or area under consideration. The fire load may consist of both the building (to the extent it is combustible) and the combustible contents. #7

Obviously, different building uses have different fire load characteristics; and, therefore, we have a variable fire problem. The designation of occupancies into groups having similar occupancy characteristics is common to most model building codes; and, with few exceptions, occupancies can be identified under the following classifications:

Classification of Building Occupancies

1. Residential
2. Educational     Low Hazard Group
3. Institutional     Fire Load 0 to 10 psf*
4. Assembly

5. Business     Medium Hazard Group
6. Mercantile     Fire Load 10 to 20 psf
*table continued on next page*

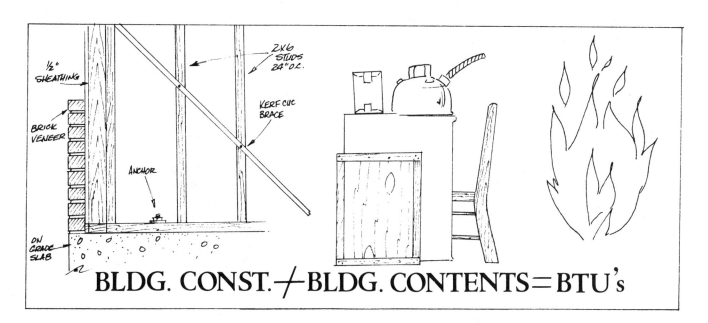

BLDG. CONST. + BLDG. CONTENTS = BTU's

7. Industrial      High Hazard Group
8. Storage       Fire Load over 20 psf
9. Hazardous

*psf - - fuel per square foot (lbs.)

Current data available for residential, educational, institutional, assembly, and business occupancies indicates that the furnishings and movable contents offer little fuel upon which a fire can feed. In these occupancies the movable contents will average about 5 pounds of fuel per square foot (psf) of floor area. This is not to say that the fire load in some areas will not exceed the 5 psf figure. If the building is of combustible construction, the available fuel represented by the framing, floors, roofs, partitions, and so forth, may run up to 15 psf of floor area (or more). Obviously, determination of the fuel load in a given area(s) may appear to be difficult, yet we can estimate the fire load of a particular building, within certain parameters.

**Effects on Tactics:** Both the intensity and duration of a fire depend on the amount of fuel contributed by the building contents and its construction materials. As stated at the outset of this section, fire load data has been derived from studies made some years ago and is considered to be conservative by present occupancy standards. If one considers the amount of synthetic materials (plastics, for example) used in the building industry today, this is a valid assumption.

A fire officer needs to consider not only the hazards associated with the combustible contents, fire loading, etc., but also the effect these hazards may have on fire fighting operations, fire fighting personnel, and above all, the occupants of the building.

# 7. Heat and Smoke

Checking fire extension requires a knowledge of how fire spreads, coupled with a knowledge of building construction features and the effects of concealed spaces, both vertical and horizontal. Whenever and wherever openings are made, hoselines should be ready. While every effort should be made to minimize damage to the building and its contents, openings have to be large enough for inspection, hose manipulation, and ventilation.

Until determined otherwise, it is a safe assumption that where you have a working fire inside a building, fire has entered concealed vertical channels.

Personnel should be looking for indicators such as:
* blisters
* discolorations on walls
* smoke patterns at moulding
* walls hot to the touch
* smoke (or fire) showing around roof features, such as vent pipes, etc.

If these are present, checking vertical extension is a must.

Even though there is a tendency for most fires to travel vertically, it does not preclude horizontal travel; and fire will follow any path available:
* void spaces between ceilings and floors
* over false or hanging ceilings
* cutwork
* utility conduits, etc.

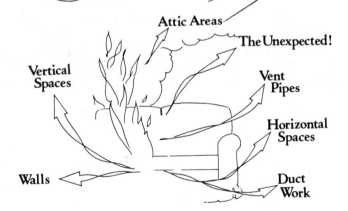

Extension occurs not only within the structure, but also from building to building. Here again, hoselines should be in place prior to opening enclosed spaces. In more cases than not, the indicators of fire in enclosed spaces are difficult to read; but you can look for some of the similar indicators present in vertical spread. Fires in concealed spaces should not be overlooked and have been responsible for fatalities, injuries and significant property loss.

12

**Effects on Tactics:** Tactical operations in large and complex occupancies will have to be carefully coordinated in order to accomplish a reduction or change in heat and smoke travel. Ventilation is a key tactical operation that will affect how, when, and where the heat and smoke spreads through a structure.

In your pre-fire inspections and plans, always look at all the possibilities of heat and smoke travel in a specific occupancy. The scene of the fire is not the place to study heat and smoke probabilities.

<u>Think ahead and be smart!</u>

Remember those fire fighter survival factors:
* **knowledge**
* **skill**
* **experience**

# 8. Fire Gases

**Gases:** Many gases found in fire buildings have a vapor density greater than 1.0, meaning they are heavier than air at normal temperatures and would normally be found near the floor. However, because gases become lighter as they are heated, the gases tend to rise and expand. Most of the gases encountered in a fire building are hot because they are products of combustion; therefore, the greatest concentration of these gases is likely to be located in the upper portions of a fire room. If the fire is extinguished <u>without</u> <u>complete ventilation</u>, the heavy, heated gases will cool and return to the lower levels during overhaul. This phenomenon proves the necessity for continued use of protective breathing apparatus and ventilation.

You should remember that a fire means exposure to combinations of the irritants and toxicants that cannot be predicted accurately beforehand. In fact, the combination can have a <u>synergistic effect</u> in which the combined effect of two or more substances is more toxic or more irritating than if each were inhaled separately.

Inhaled toxic gases may have several harmful effects on the human body. Some of the gases directly cause disease of the lung tissue and impair its function. Other gases have no direct harmful effect on the lungs but pass into the bloodstream and to other parts of the body and impair the oxygen-carrying capacity of the red blood cells.

The particular toxic gases given off at a fire vary according to four factors:
 - The nature of the combustible product
 - The rate of heating
 - The temperature of the evolving gases
 - The oxygen concentration

It would be impossible to list all fire gases that exhibit toxic effects. Also, it would be impractical because the amounts present and the doses inhaled, ingested, or absorbed vary so widely. Therefore, no attempt has been made to record the exact dose necessary to cause harmful effects. Rather, the gases listed are the ones most commonly produced.

**Carbon Monoxide:** More fire deaths occur from carbon monoxide (CO) than from any other toxic product of combustion. This colorless, tasteless, poisonous, flammable gas is present with every fire; and the poorer the ventilation and the more inefficient the burning, the greater the quantity of carbon monoxide formed. A rule of thumb, although subject to variation, is that darker smoke means higher carbon monoxide levels. Black smoke is high in particulate carbon and carbon monoxide because of incomplete combustion.

The blood's hemoglobin combines with and carries oxygen in a loose chemical combination called oxyhemoglobin. The most significant characteristic of carbon monoxide is that it combines with the blood's hemoglobin so readily that the available oxygen is excluded. The loose combination of oxyhemoglobin becomes a strong combination called carboxyhemoglobin (COHb). In fact, carbon monoxide combines with hemoglobin about 200 times more readily than does oxygen. The carbon monoxide does not act on the body but crowds oxygen from the blood and leads to eventual hypoxia of the brain and tissues, followed by death if the process is not reversed.

Concentration of carbon monoxide in the air of about five hundredths of one percent (0.05 percent) can be dangerous. When the level is more than one

percent, there is no sensory warning in time to allow escape. At lower levels, there is headache and dizziness before incapacitation, so sufficient warning is possible. The characteristic cherry-red skin color of carbon monoxide poisoning is not always a reliable sign, particularly in long exposures to low concentrations.

Measurements of carbon monoxide concentrations in air are not the best way to predict rapid physiological effects because the actual reaction is from the concentration of carboxyhemoglobin in the blood causing oxygen starvation. High oxygen users, such as the heart and brain, are damaged early. The entry of carbon monoxide into the blood will be greater when its concentration in the air is higher.

An individual's general physical condition, age, degree of physical activity, and length of exposure all affect the actual carboxyhemoglobin level in the blood.

Experiments have provided some comparison relating air and blood concentrations to carbon monoxide. A one percent concentration of carbon monoxide in a room will cause a fifty percent level of carboxyhemoglobin in the bloodstream in two-and-one-half to seven minutes. A five percent concentration can elevate carboxyhemoglobin levels to fifty percent in only 30 to 90 seconds. Because the newly formed carboxyhemoglobin may be traveling through the body, a person previously exposed to a high level of carbon monoxide may react later in a safer atmosphere. A person so exposed should not be allowed to use breathing apparatus or resume fire control activities until the danger of toxic reaction has passed. Even with protection, a firefighter may become unconscious in a toxic atmosphere.

A hardworking firefighter may be incapacitated by a one percent concentration of carbon monoxide. The stable combination of carbon monoxide with the blood is only slowly eliminated by normal breathing. Administering pure oxygen is the most important element in the first aid care. After an uneventful convalescence from a severe exposure, signs of nerve or brain injury may appear any time within three weeks. Again, this is a reason why an overcome firefighter who quickly revives should still not be allowed to re-enter a smoky atmosphere.

**Hyrdogen Chloride:** Hydrogen Chloride (HCL) is colorless but is easily detected by its pungent odor and intense irritation to the eyes and respiratory tract. Although not a general poison, hydrogen chloride causes swelling and obstruction of the upper respiratory tract. Breathing is labored and suffocation can result. This gas is more commonly present in fires because of the increased use of plastics such as polyvinyl chloride (PVC) containing chlorine.

In addition to the usual presence of plastics in homes, fire fighters can expect to encounter plastics containing chlorine in drug, toy, and general merchandise stores. The overhaul stage is especially dangerous because breathing apparatus is often removed, and toxic fumes linger in a room. Heated concrete can remain hot enough to decompose the plastics in telephone or electrical cable and release more hydrogen chloride.

**Hydrogen Cyanide:** Hydrogen Cyanide (HCN) interferes with respiration at the cellular and tissue level. The proper exchange of oxygen and carbon dioxide is hampered so hydrogen cyanide is classified as a chemical asphyxiant. The gas inhibits the enzymes in the tissues which take up oxygen. Hydrogen cyanide also can be absorbed through the skin.

Materials that give off hydrogen cyanide include wool, polyurethane foam, rubber and paper. Hazardous HCN atmospheres might be found at fires in clothing stores or rug shops. Exposure to this colorless gas that has a noticeable almond odor might cause gasping respirations, muscle spasms, and increased heart rate, possibly up to 100 beats per minute. Collapse is often sudden. An atmosphere containing 135 parts per million (.0125 percent) is fatal within 30 minutes; a concentration of .0270 ppm is fatal. Nearly all materials tested in an experiment with aircraft interior materials yielded some hydrogen cyanide.

**Carbon Dioxide:** Carbon dioxide ($CO_2$) must be considered because it is an end product of the complete combustion of carbonnaceous materials. Carbon dioxide is nonflammable, colorless and odorless. Free-burning fires generally form more carbon dioxide than do smoldering fires. Normally, its presence in air and its exchange from the bloodstream into the lungs stimulates the respiratory center of the brain. Air normally contains about 0.03 percent carbon

dioxide. With a five percent concentration, there is a marked increase in respiration along with headache, dizziness, sweating, and mental excitement. Concentrations of ten or twelve percent cause death within a few minutes from paralysis of the brain's respiratory center. Unfortunately, increased breathing increases the inhalation of other toxic gases. As the gas increases, the initially stimulated breathing rate becomes depressed before a total paralysis takes place.

Fire fighters should anticipate high carbon dioxide levels when a carbon dioxide total flooding system has been activated. These systems are designed to extinguish a fire by excluding the oxygen, and they will have the same effect on a fire fighter. According to the American Conference of Industrial Hygenists, exposure for even a short time to carbon dioxide concentrations greater than 15,000 ppm should be avoided.

**Nitrogen Oxides:** There are two dangerous oxides of nitrogen: nitrogen dioxide and nitric oxide. Nitrogen dioxide is the most significant because nitric oxide readily converts to nitrogen dioxide in the presence of oxygen and moisture. Nitrogen dioxide is a pulmonary irritant that has a reddish-brown color. When inhaled in sufficient concentrations, it causes pulmonary edema that blocks the body's natural respiration processes and leads to death by suffocation.

In addition, all oxides of nitrogen are soluble in water and react in the presence of oxygen to form nitric and nitrous acids. These acids are neutralized by the alkalies in the body tissues and form nitrites and nitrates. These substances chemically attach to the blood and can lead to collapse and coma. Nitrates and nitrites can also cause arterial dilation, variation in blood pressure, headaches, and dizziness. The effects of nitrites and nitrates are secondary to the irritant effects of nitrogen dioxide but can become important under certain circumstances when they cause delayed physical reactions.

Nitrogen dioxide is an insidious gas because its irritable effects in the nose and throat can be tolerated even though a lethal dose is being inhaled. Therefore, its hazardous effects from its pulmonary irritation action or chemical reaction may not become apparent for several hours after exposure.

**Phosgene:** Phosgene (COCL2) is a colorless, tasteless gas with a disagreeable odor. It may be produced when refrigerants, such as freon, contact flame. It is a strong lung irritant, and its full poisonous effect is not evident for several hours after exposure. The musty-hay odor of phosgene is perceptible at 6 ppm, although lesser amounts cause coughing and eye irritation. Twenty-five ppm is deadly. When phosgene contacts water, it decomposes into hydrochloric acid. Because the lungs and bronchial tubes are always moist, phosgene forms hydrochoric acid in the lungs when inhaled.

## The Hazards of Working a Contaminated Atmosphere

**Carcinogenic Effect of Fire Gases:** There are many toxic substances found in the smoke and heated gases which are produced by a fire. An often overlooked problem with these substances is not their short-term effects but rather their long-term effects.

To better understand the long-term effects of toxic substances, it is best to divide them into two categories: carcinogens and immunosuppressants. A carcinogen is any substance that is believed to be a cancer-causing agent. Firefighters are routinely exposed to these carcinogens; but, if proper precautions are taken, they too can reduce the risk of lethal doses of these substances. Among the substances found in smoke, building materials, and gasoline are the following known or suspected carcinogens:

> Formaldehyde
> Benzol (A) Pyrene
> Polycyclic Hydrocarbons
> Asbestos
> Lead
> Wood dust
> Methylene Dichloride
> Ethylene Dibromide
> Nitrosamines.

The course of carcinogens can be followed with the equation:

$$\text{Susceptibility} + \text{Carcinogens} + \text{Cofactors} \overset{(TIME)}{=} \text{CANCER}$$

Susceptibility may also depend on an individual's own heredity or family history of cancer and also exposure to immunosuppressants. A

**15**

carcinogen's effect can also depend on its potency and an individual's duration of exposure. Cofactors which can effect the lethality of carcinogens include age, sex, race, obesity, skin complexion, heat sensitivity, tobacco and alcohol use, and exposure to radiant energy, such as ultrviolet light, sunlight, and X-rays.

In addition to carcinogens, many substances encountered on a fire scene include immunosuppressants, which, while they do not directly cause cancer, suppress the immune system so much that an individual becomes susceptible to not only cancer but many other diseases. Examples of known or suspected immunosuppressants are the following:

Formaldehyde
Chlorine
Carbon Monoxide
Hydrogen Chloride
Acrolein
Oxides of Nitrogen
Acetaldehyde
Acetic Acid
Benzo (A) Pyrene
Formic Acid
Polycyclic Hydrocarbons
Hydrogen Cyanide
Phosgene
Alcohol

The length of time it takes for a carcinogen to cause cancer or an immunosuppressant to damage the immune system varies greatly, from a few months to many years; therefore, fire fighters must exercise utmost caution and remember the many detrimental effects of these toxic substances.

**Effects on Tactics:** Initial tactical operations may be impacted when there is a hazardous material involved producing a significant amount of highly toxic fire gases. Additionally, fires involving select materials, such as plastic, rubber and wood (just to name a few), will also require you to assess your initial attack procedures. However, in the normal structure fire adequate protection can be afforded by :
*The use of full protective equipment
*The use of an SCBA during initial fire attack and through the overhaul process
*Decontamination of personnel and equipment after each fire

## 9. Thermal Stratification

*Thermal stratification is the layering of heat in a given enclosed area. The ceiling or upper areas will be a higher temperature. The floor covering materials are potentially less hazardous than ceiling or wall surfaces.*

In the pre-fire inspection, you should not ignore the degree of combustibility of materials used throughout the occupancy. In the MGM Grand Hotel fire, the use of plastic materials in ceiling areas impacted dramatically on the fire behavior.

**Effects on Tactics:** The introduction of water into a room, through a nozzle, will rapidly change the thermal stratification of the enclosed area. In most cases, there will be a thermal balance occurring, following the induction of water. The temperature in the room will equalize.

If the thermal balance is disturbed, temperatures can be raised beyond the point where any victims trapped inside would have a chance of surviving. Wide fogs applied into a room can turn the water into super-heated steam endangering both potential victims and fire fighters. Full protective clothing and SCBA are a must if the safety of fire fighters is to be protected.

## 10. Weather Conditions

Weather will have a pronounced effect on fire behavior and the ability to perform tactical operations.

**16**

**Extreme Heat:** Temperatures in excess of 100 degrees F° will accelerate the ignition temperature of combustibles. This high heat will also dramatically affect the ability of fire fighters to perform tactical evaluations over extended time periods. Be on guard for heat stress problems among fire fighters in excessive heat climates. Tactical operations will require additional personnel.

**Extreme Cold:** Temperatures below 32 degrees F° also will affect fire behavior. Normally, the humidity is much lower and combustibles will ignite more readily. Water flows need to be controlled so that supply lines are not frozen before attack lines are in place. Tactical operations will take longer, and personnel protection from the cold elements must be considered. Additional resources will be necessary to accomplish many standard tactical functions.

**High Winds:** Winds in excess of 25 mph will affect the fire behavior and spread heat and smoke rapidly. Many past conflagrations have been in high wind conditions. Fires will spread quickly through combustibles in structures where openings are located on the windward side. Normally, the humidity is lower in high winds. High winds also have an effect on the chill factor in extreme cold temperatures and thus reduce fire fighter tactical operations.

**Low Humidity:** Low humidity affects all materials and increases the probability of ignition. A good example is wild land fuel (and grass) moisture analysis. When the fuel moisture gets below 60 percent, the fire hazard is considered critical. Combustibles will ignite and flame spread will be greater in low humidity.

Low humidity will also impact the performance of firefighters. Again, heat stress and over-exertion are problems.

**High Humidity:** Climatic conditions of high humidity will reduce the ignition potential of most combustibles. High humidity dramatically affects wildland fire conditions. In addition, high humidity can have a serious effect on fire fighters' physical endurance while performing tactical operations.

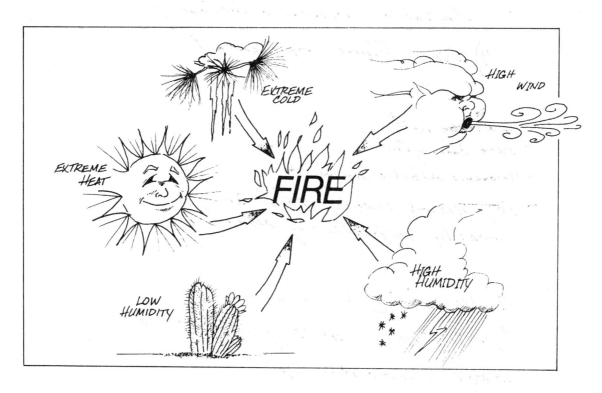

# Fire Behavior
## * * STUDENT ACTIVITY * *

1. List five fire behavior factors that are an important part of a fire officer's size-up.

    1) Heat Release      weather

    2) " Transfer     Heat + Smoke Travel

    3) FlasLover

    4) Back oraf

    5) Fire Load

2. There are three basic methods by which heat from the combustion of materials is transferred. List and explain all three.

    1) Conduction (Throgh a mediun)

    2) Convection (By means of Circulation)

    3) Radiation (without a medium)

    4) Direct Flame impingement.

3. You are making entry on a residential structure fire. What signs would indicate to you that conditions for a flashover exist?

    - Intense Heat
    - Free Burning Fire
    - Unburned particles smoking
    - Fog Streams turning to Steam shortly after leaving Nozzle

4. Explain what a backdraft is:

    Intro of $O_2$ to confino Space that's under pressurized w/ heated Flammable Gases

    Pg 8

**18**

5. You are the first officer on the scene of a structure fire that indicates a possible backdraft condition. What are your tactical objectives?

*To perform verticle ventilation with lines in place and assuring fire fighters safety*

6. Define ignition temperature:

*Pg 10*

7. Explain fire load:

*Pg 11*

8. What is (psf)?

*Pounds of fuel per sq ft.*

9. You are a company officer on an engine company. Your company has been assigned to check for fire extension on the second and third floors of a three-story apartment house, which has had a fire on the first floor. Where would you look?

*2nd + 3rd floor verticle channels*

*Pg 12*

10. Explain the necessity for using breathing apparatus during the overhaul phase of a fire.

*Product of Comb. still present and in fact Beginning to collect @ lower levels*

11. Many contaminants present on the fireground during firefighting operations are called immunosuppresants. Explain what they are.

*Pg 16*

12. Explain thermal stratification:

*Layering*

*Pg 16*

13. It is 95°F with winds of 25 to 30 mph when you are called to a reported structure fire. How will those weather conditions effect:

   1) Fire behavior

   *Conflagaration Potential Pre heated Dry fuel loads*

   *Pg 17.*

   2) Tactical operations

   *↑ Manpower. ↑ Effects on physical Endurance*

   *Pg 17*

# MODULE TWO

## SUCCESSFUL SCENE MANAGEMENT

# VIDEO NOTES

_____

_____

_____

_____

_____

_____

_____

_____

_____

_____

_____

_____

_____

_____

_____

_____

_____

_____

_____

_____

_____

_____

# SUCCESSFUL SCENE MANAGEMENT

Many experienced fire officers will tell you there are three phases to managing an emergency incident. Those three phases are:

    1. Panic
    2. Confusion
    3. Remorse

Many will also argue that the third phase should be fixing blame, while others contend that a strong legal defense deserves consideration.

If you are looking for an alternative to Panic, Confusion, and Remorse, we offer these three steps to successful incident management:

    **1. Think**
    **2. Plan**
    **3. Act**

## Think

The first step is the hardest--THINK! The usual excuse one hears is, "You don't have time to think at an emergency. It's a time for action, not deep thought." The other excuse often heard for not taking the time to first think before acting is, "It makes my head hurt."

Thinking doesn't have to hurt. There is a wealth of information available to help get the thought process started. That's the information you have before the alarm ever sounds. It includes your departmental pre-fire plans. They allow you to become familiar with the problems you can anticipate in your target hazards and the solutions to deal with those problems. Within your company or within your department, pre-fire plans can serve as a great training tool. Different problems can be presented for a given pre-planned hazard, and the methods you would use for control can be worked out either in a classroom skull session or on-site training exercise. If you are lucky, during one of your training sessions you may have already fought the fire in one of your pre-planned target hazards.

Other information you already have, or can easily acquire, is the general knowledge of what is out there in your first response area or district. When the call comes in, the address should give you an indication of what you are responding to. By becoming familiar with your response area, you should be able to narrow the concerns you may be facing. What is the type of neighborhood? Residential, commercial, industrial? Is it an area with a good water supply or will water be a problem? What is the typical construction in that area? Is it fire resistive, ordinary, Styrofoam? Is it an older area or a newer area built under more recent codes? What's the occupancy? Is it a school, home for the criminally insane? Does it have a sprinkler or stand-pipe system? What is the time of day and what are the weather conditions? Best response route? What other companies are responding? Other agencies or resources available? What about building contents? Anvil warehouse or fireworks?

Anytime you are out and about in your area, you can be making observations that may well be invaluable during emergency conditions. Take particular note of those occupancies, hazards, or unusual conditions

that may present particular problems. This is the type of information you can keep filed in the back of your mind that will help you to identify the problems and their solutions while controlling the incident.

The toughest time to get the brain engaged is when you are looking out through the windshield of your vehicle at a display of chaos and confusion. Your on-scene size-up should be a rapid but thorough analysis of what you see. This process should start with some basic understandings. Almost without exception, we respond to someone else's mistake. We must remind ourselves that, "It's not my fault. I didn't start it." Your first step should be to take a moment to GYST. In polite circles, this can stand for Get YourSelf Together. The purpose of GYST is to get yourself calmed down so that you can take an objective look at what is going on. An officer must be detached and not get caught up in the excitement an incident can cause.

There are several methods already developed to assist you in making your size-up. Whatever method works best for you should help you determine: 1) What exactly is going on here? and 2) Now what do I need to do? The flames may be turning the clouds to steam, but don't let them demand all of your attention until you have determined what other problems may exist. The fire may be putting on a spectacular display; but your real problem may be one of rescue, perhaps exposures, or a variety of others in addition to the fire. After the problems have been identified, they are prioritized as to the order in which they need to be addressed.

## Size-Up

The size-up should be an orderly process that ensures that the officer considers:
* the factors necessary to identify the problems
* the priority order in which they need to be addressed
* the resources needed
* how those resources can best be utilized.

With any incident, we know that our first priority is the protection of lives. Our second priority is to stabilize and control the incident, and our third priority is the conservation and preservation of property. This should also be the priority order we should follow in doing our size-up.

To assist in following an orderly thought process, we have enlisted the assistance of an old Indian chief who was also the tribe's fire chief. Back in the days prior to large diameter hose and SCBAs, Chief REVAS followed a simple pattern of doing a size-up when fires occurred within the tribal circle. Like most of us, Chief REVAS was able to maintain the ability to remember his name during times of high stress such as found when showing up at a fire. Using his own name, Chief REVAS followed these steps when looking at the fire and doing his size-up:

By following these steps at every incident, Chief REVAS addressed the priorities of LIFE SAFETY, INCIDENT STABILIZATION, and PROPERTY CONSERVATION in their proper order when doing his size-up. We will use these same steps throughout this course to help us answer the questions: (1) What exactly is going on here? and (2) Now what do I need to do?

An important part of your size-up should include a forecast of probable spread of the incident. This might be applying the principles discussed in Module I to make a fire behavior prediction, assessing the threat of toxic materials at a haz-mat incident, or establishing a system to control and account for victims evacuated

**24**

from a building. By making a forecast, you will be better able to determine what future actions may need to be taken and the resources you will need.

In addition to your evaluation of the incident, you should evaluate your available resources. Do you have enough personnel and the right personnel? Your need may be for more fire fighters or it may be for more command officers. The incident may require those with specialized knowledge or skills. Do you have enough apparatus and equipment, and is it what you need? If you have lost the structure and are into an aerial stream operation, your need is likely to be for more aerial ladders rather than engines. The incident may require large amounts of foam or breathing air beyond that available at the scene. Consider additional crews for attack, the need for relief personnel, the need for additional water, and the need for additional or specialized apparatus and equipment. The danger is attempting to do too much with the resources at hand, only to find out too late they were insufficient or the wrong ones to meet the challenge. This can risk the safety of your personnel and put you in a catch-up mode throughout the incident.

## On-Scene Report

For the first arriving officer, the initial size-up should include a complete on-scene report. If that officer can communicate a graphic word picture as to what is occurring at the incident, other incoming units will have a better understanding of what the incident is, which will reduce the confusion once they arrive. One method used by a number of departments is that the officer communicates the answers to the following questions:

> What do I have?
> What am I doing?
> What do I need?
> Who is in command?

In describing "WHAT DO I HAVE?" the officer gives the communications center and other responding units an image of what the officer sees. The description can include such information as building size, construction, amount of smoke or flame showing, amount of involvement, type of occupancy, unusual

conditions or hazards, or any other information the officer can give. This brief report will help others picture what is occurring.

"WHAT AM I DOING?" will tell them what actions you are taking such as advancing an attack line, supplying your own water, laddering the building, or whatever your initial actions might be.

"WHAT DO I NEED?" can be assignments you give to other companies or request for additional resources. When telling others what your needs are, remember that "nothing right now" is a perfectly good answer. You may need time to do some investigation to determine what the real problems are. While you are taking the time to determine what is wrong, other responding units can be directed to stage in an area close to the incident but far enough away to easily be placed somewhere other than the front door. All too often, the front of a building looks like a used fire apparatus lot when everyone stacks up in front of the front door. Keeping apparatus away until they are needed allows for easier access if apparatus needs to be moved in or out.

One question that has to be answered on every incident is, "WHO IS IN COMMAND?" Once the first piece of fire equipment arrives at the scene and until the last one leaves, someone has to be in command. Everyone responding to or working at an incident needs to know that command is established. Your department should have SOPs dealing with how command is established and transferred.

In size-up as well as all your other actions, personnel safety is the officer's number one responsibility. The risks to which an officer exposes personnel must be weighed against the benefits. Don't risk the lives of fire fighters in a vain attempt to save dead people or in an aggressive interior attack on a building not worth saving. You must be able and willing to assess when the risk is not worth the benefit.

## Plan

The second step to successful incident management is to PLAN. Based on the information the IC was able to develop in the THINK step, problems were:

1) identified
2) they were prioritized
3) a forecast made as to probable spread
4) resources were evaluated, and the safety of the personnel considered.

Now the IC is able to establish the plan or strategy to control the incident. The plan should address two questions:

1. What has to be done?
2. How is it going to be done?

**Goals:** In answering the question, "<u>WHAT HAS TO BE DONE</u>?" the IC will determine what the goals are for the incident. Webster defines a goal as "the end to which a person aims to reach or accomplish." To the IC, goals determine what needs to be accomplished. Examples could be to rescue victims trapped above fire floor, effect ventilation, or protect exposures.

**Objectives:** The answer to "<u>HOW WILL IT BE DONE?</u>" will establish the objectives which the IC will set to attain the incident goals. According to Webster, objectives are "those specific actions carried out to accomplish goals." If goals are the "end," then objectives are the paths that lead to that end. If one of the goals set by the IC is to rescue victims trapped above the fire, several objectives may need to be met to effectively accomplish that goal. One objective may be to confine the fire to provide an escape route for the victims, another to assign rescue crews to effect the rescue, and a third might be to ventilate the structure to clear smoke and gases to reduce the danger to trapped victims and to aid fire fighting and rescue efforts.

The PLAN will set the direction everyone will work toward and gives the IC a gauge by which success of the efforts can be judged. Knee-jerk fire fighting is seeing flame, then taking the "wet stuff" and throwing it at the "red stuff" without first taking the time to think and plan. This puts us in a reactive mode, reacting to what we see rather than having thought our actions through. Fire fighters as a group are aggressive by nature, and our first instinct is to take <u>immediate</u> action.

# Act

Only after you have gone through the THINK and

PLAN steps are you ready to take the third step in successful incident management. That third step is to ACT. In the ACT step, the IC assigns the tactics to meet objectives. The IC should caution against becoming too involved in tactics. If the IC becomes too involved, there is the distinct possibility of exceeding span of control and losing an overall perspective of the incident and going into overload. If this occurs, personnel safety is at risk and coordination of the tactical operation is lost.

When implementing your plan, there may be a tendency to wish things to happen faster than reality will allow. An IC needs to recognize that giving an order and the order being carried out are two different things. Your planning should reflect how the tactics are going to impact at the time when they are carried out, not when the orders are given. As has been said, "Don't fight the fire you see, fight it where it will be."

You may be the first ever to come up with the absolutely perfect plan; but, unless you are able to communicate the plan to others, you could end up in the toilet. Don't load up your messages with a bunch of garbage. Learn to get the information to others in as clear and concise a manner as possible, keeping your verbage to a minimum. The best way to learn how to do an effective job of communicating is to train in a non-stress environment and not use the fireground as your practice field. Train in the classroom; then put it into practice on the fireground.

To a great degree, how well the plan works will reflect in the IC's ability to coordinate the tactics being carried out at the incident. If a backdraft potential exists, the IC should order ventilation to be done in coordination with attack lines. What the IC must understand is that it takes longer to set up and accomplish ventilation than it does to pull a hand line and kick in a door to make an attack. If the IC doesn't see to it that the two operations are properly timed and coordinated, fire fighters may be placed in serious jeopardy. It takes about the same amount of time to give most orders, but how quickly they can be carried out may vary greatly. It is the IC's job to coordinate the incident so that companies are working toward the same goals, personnel safety is protected, and the spread of the incident is kept to a minimum.

When implementing your plan, if there is any question in your mind as to whether you need

26

additional resources, the answer is most often, "Yes." Don't wait until your need for assistance is immediate to request additional resources. At that point, they had better already be there or well on their way.

Another important point to remember is that you are not the only one there with a plan. The fire also has a plan and that is to burn the structure down. Some days the fire can have a better plan than the one you first came up with. While it is true that all fire fighters are honest, fair, and straightforward, the fire doesn't always play by the same rules. Fires can cheat, keep secrets and deceive you. This means the IC must be ready to modify the plan if the fire isn't playing fair and going out.

Emergency scenes are dynamic, not static; and the IC must be prepared to be flexible. Several factors may require changes or modifications in the plan. The first and most obvious indicator is if you now have more fire and less building, things probably aren't going all that well. When you initiate the attack, you may very well be operating with limited information. As the scene progresses, more information may become available which will require changes in your plan.

The good news is that everything may be going like clockwork and the initial goals you established are being met. This is the time to set new goals or objectives which deal with the demobilization phase of the incident. Some officers forget that managing an incident goes beyond gaining control. The incident must be well managed from start to finish, and we don't get to quit in the middle when the fun stuff like throwing water and rescuing babies is over.

The theory is that if you do everything right in the THINK, PLAN and ACT steps, the fire will go out. If life were fair, that would be the case. In the real world, life sometimes just isn't all that fair. If you are convinced your plan is of world-class caliber and the fire rages on, don't beat a dead horse or continue with a plan that's not working. A good officer assumes "Plan A" isn't going to work and tries to anticipate where the plan could go wrong, what actions will be required if it does, and what resources will be needed. This allows you to quickly modify the plan if changes need to be made.

Having a plan for every incident allows you to protect the safety of your people and maximize the effectiveness of your resources. If you only plan at "the big ones," you most likely will not have established the habits needed to do a complete and effective job of planning. Things fall through the cracks, people get hurt, and buildings burn down. Captain Marvelous wouldn't let that happen . . . "DON'T YOU!"

# The Incident Command System

## Introduction

Once upon a time there was a fire department; and every time an emergency incident occurred, the officer at the scene made all the decisions and gave all the orders. This department was known throughout the land for its ability to create parking lots where proud buildings once stood. This system of managing emergencies, known as the "Operate to Best Advantage" system, has resulted in:

* Duplication of effort
* Failure to address all problems at the incident
* Improper utilization of resources
* Higher losses
* Greater risk of death and injury to fire fighters

What this department needed was a better way to manage its resources. Across this country, the fire service is being forced to become better managers. While the fire problem in America continues to grow, most departments are facing personnel and budget cutbacks, attacks on productivity levels, reductions in the hourly work week, and the demands to do more with less. In order to become better managers, a number of departments have turned to a proven emergency management system which applies principles that have been successful in business and industry for years.

Back in the early 1970s, southern California was burning down with amazing regularity. Fires burned over large areas of wildland and consumed numerous homes, many in exclusive neighborhoods in the hills behind Los Angeles. Since the fires raged across jurisdictional boundaries and involved state and federal forests, a multitude of departments and agencies were involved in trying to control the fires.

27

Lack of a common plan for emergency operations coupled with the inability of the agencies to communicate with one another through a common network lead to a variety of problems. Efforts to coordinate the vast resources committed to these large scale emergencies proved to be futile. A plan was needed to effect communication between and coordination of the resources from this wide variety of departments and agencies within the southern California region.

Representatives from a broad spectrum of agencies and jurisdictions banded together to develop an emergency management system which they called FIRESCOPE. This early system has been refined and is being used, not only nationwide, but in several foreign countries under the label of the Incident Command System (ICS). A group of agencies involved nationally in wildland fire fighting formed the National Interagency Incident Management System (NIIMS) and has modified the Incident Command System into its present form. In conjunction with Fire Service Publications at Oklahoma State University, NIIMS is producing training materials to support departments and agencies wishing to adopt ICS.

The National Fire Academy is a strong supporter of the ICS system and has made it an integral part of its curriculum in courses dealing with emergency management. Several states have designated ICS as the command system to be used on a statewide basis.

The reason ICS has gained such broad acceptance and support is simple: it works. It works at those incidents that make the headlines, and it also works every day as the standard mode of operation for a wide variety of departments all across the country on every call they run.

Some say that ICS will only work for large departments, while others maintain it is only needed at large-scale incidents. The flaw in such thinking is that small departments need to get the most out of limited resources; ICS allows them to manage their resources while maximizing their effectiveness. Of course, larger departments also have the need to maximize their resources, in addition to coordinating a large number of resources effectively during an emergency. ICS works best in those departments where it is the standard system used on every call. When an

"emergency plan" is used only during large-scale emergencies, it tends to be ineffective due to a lack of familiarity by those who must make the plan work. If ICS is used at every incident, officers and fire fighters become familiar enough with the system to use it successfully no matter how large or complex the incident.

For those who command an incident, ICS can do much to make them better managers. Most of those who have experienced the thrill of victory and the agony of command can identify with a phenomenon known as the "pucker factor." It is the affliction that strikes when you pull up to a fire with flames that appear to be only slightly higher than the World Trade Center. The major symptom is the inability to exit your vehicle due to the ironclad grip your fanny has on the vehicle's seat. A cure for this dreaded affliction can be found with ICS. It allows the incident commander (IC) to delegate responsibility and maintain span of control. It establishes clear lines of communication for the flow of information which will allow the IC to have a better overall understanding of what is occurring at the incident.

Good management is simply a matter of identifying the problems, evaluating resources, and applying those resources in an effective manner to the problems. ICS provides the management system to allow the IC to be an effective manager, thus reducing the impact the "pucker factor" can have on the IC's ability to manage an incident.

Another advantage of ICS is that it provides the opportunity for departments and agencies from a wide geographic area to work together. The organizational structure and communication network of ICS allow agencies to coordinate their efforts. Part of this coordination and communication is established in the use of clear text and standard resource designators. These designations reduce the chance for confusion and improve coordination. Experience has shown ICS will work no matter what type of emergency or number of jurisdictions involved.

The structure of ICS is divided into five functional areas that are present in varying degrees at every incident. These functional areas are:
* Command
* Operations

* Planning
* Logistics
* Finance

# Command

The first functional area is <u>COMMAND</u>, which has overall responsibility for the incident. The Incident Commander serves the function of Command and establishes the goals and objectives that all other resources will work towards accomplishing. The IC will develop, implement, monitor, and modify the action plan which others will follow to control the incident. The remaining four functional areas are under the direction of Command. In addition, the IC can create three Command Staff Officers who will also report directly to the IC. Those Command Staff positions are:

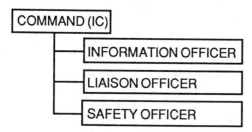

The <u>INFORMATION OFFICER</u> is responsible for formulation and release of incident information to the media and other appropriate agencies. The Information Officer can satisfy the media's need for information while allowing the IC to concentrate on managing the incident without having the distraction of dealing with the media.

The <u>LIAISON</u> OFFICER is the point of contact for assisting and coodinating outside agency representatives. When several agencies are involved at one incident, there is often a lack of communication and coordination between the agencies. The Liaison Officer's role is to provide that communication and coordination to insure there is no duplication of effort and all available resources are used to fullest capabilities.

The <u>SAFETY OFFICER</u> is responsible for monitoring and assessing hazards or unsafe situations and developing measures for assuring personnel safety. The Safety Officer keeps the IC informed of present or potential hazards so that the IC can build

personnel safety into the action plan. The Safety Officer can take immediate steps to correct any unsafe act or remove personnel from imminent danger.

# Operations

<u>OPERATIONS</u> is the functional area responsible for all the tactical operations carried out to meet the goals and objectives established by the IC.

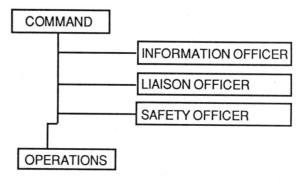

If the IC is the overall commander, the Operations Chief can be considered the field commander directing the troops in their efforts to accomplish the IC's plan. The Operations Chief's role is to command and coordinate the efforts of divisions or groups.

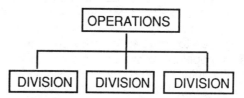

<u>DIVISIONS</u> are made up of resources that operate in a defined area and are usually designated numerically or geographically; i.e., Division 3, Division North, etc. <u>Groups are functional divisions</u> that are responsible for a specific function and are designated by their function; i.e., Ventilation Group, Medical Group, etc. At most incidents, companies or teams are assigned to a group or division in numbers that allow for meeting the objectives while still maintaining span of control by the division or group supervisor. At larger incidents where significant resources are available, task forces or strike teams consisting of several companies or resources can be assigned to a division or group.

If the number of divisions or groups exceeds the

29

Operations Chief's span of control, BRANCHES can be established. For example:

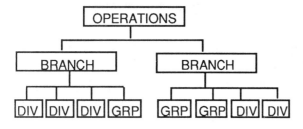

A manageable number of divisions or groups can be assigned to each branch allowing the Operations Chief to regain span of control.

Another part of Operations is STAGING. Staging is under the control of the Operations Chief and is where unassigned resources report.

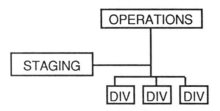

The STAGING AREA is located close to the incident, yet far away enough so as not to interfere with emergency operations. Rather than incoming units calling for assignments prior to arrival, such units report to the Staging Area to await assignment until they are needed. This reduces the amount of "free-lance fire fighting" or companies being given an assignment just to get them off someone's back. By being in the Staging Area, waiting units are ready for immediate assignment should

1) modification of the action plan be necessary
2) additional resources may be needed in areas where the objectives are not being met
3) new objectives have been established requiring additional resources
4) there is a need to provide relief for crews already engaged.

# Planning

The next functional area is PLANNING.

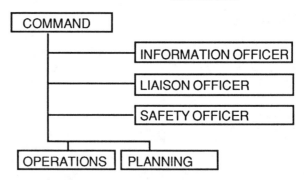

PLANNING is responsible for the gathering and assimilation of information in two primary areas. These areas are Situation Status and Resource Status.

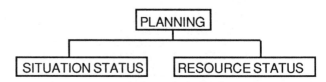

SITUATION STATUS is the gathering of information regarding the incident itself. The Plans Chief should gather as much information as possible on what has happened at the incident, the effectiveness of current operations in dealing with the emergency, and a forecast as to the probable or possible spread of the incident.

RESOURCE STATUS is the gathering of information on the resources currently at the incident, how they are deployed, and how effectively they are being utilized. In addition, a projection of any additional resources needs to be made.

Based on evaluation of the Situation Status and Resource Status, the Plans Chief is able to make recommendations to the IC concerning modifications to the action plan. The need for additional resources as well as consideration to release current on- scene resources are further areas of evaluation.

## Logistics

LOGISTICS is the next functional area of ICS.

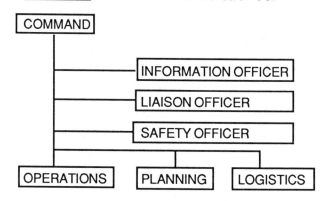

LOGISTICS is responsible for providing the facilities, services, and supplies to support the incident. Logistics is broken down into two major areas of responsibility:

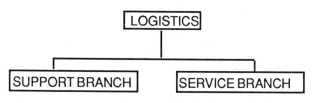

The SERVICE BRANCH is responsible for incident communications, providing medical aid for emergency personnel, and for feeding the personnel at the incident.

The SUPPORT BRANCH is responsible for ordering and storing all supplies, providing any facilities or shelter needed, and for ground support such as fuel or maintenance.

## Finance

The fifth functional area is that of FINANCE.

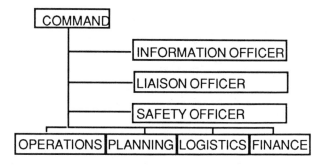

FINANCE is responsible for all financial aspects of the incident. The Finance Chief oversees personnel costs, costs to contractors or vendors, claims due to injuries, and monitoring the legalities with regards to finance.

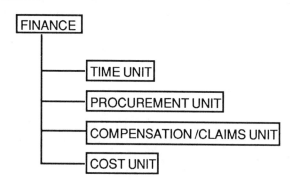

## Summary

At first glance, ICS can appear to be somewhat complex and overpowering. To help simplify the system we can look at ICS in two ways. First, if you look at the ICS organizational chart as a job description, the IC is responsible for filling any and all of the jobs needing to be done at an incident until those jobs can be delegated to others. This gives the IC some incentive to know and understand the system so that an effective job of delegation can be done to allow the IC to maintain span of control.

Secondly, we can look at ICS as a toolbox filled with tools. Each tool represents a resource the IC has available should the need arise. The IC needs only to select the right tool to do the job most effectively. When you do a tune-up on your car, you don't need every tool you own. Only those necessary to get the job done properly are needed. The tools you don't need remain in the tool box until you do a job where they are needed. The same is true of the ICS organization. You only need to fill those positions which will help you get the job done in a manner that maximizes the effectiveness of available resources and protects the safety of personnel.

How ICS is implemented can be affected by the knowledge and abilities of the Incident Commander, the resources available, or both. If the IC is experienced and confident in his/her ability to manage the incident, their span of control may be broader than a less experienced officer. An example might be a haz-

31

mat incident in which the IC has a limited background in dealing with incidents of this type, while another officer at the scene has extensive training in the control of hazardous materials. In this case, the IC may wish to appoint the officer with the greater training as Operations Chief to handle the tactics needed to control the incident. If, however, the IC is comfortable dealing with a haz-mat situation, the position of Operations Chief may never be filled.

If the IC has limited resources available, the ability to fill positions within the ICS structure is restricted. The greater the number of resources the IC has to manage, the greater the opportunity the IC has to delegate positions. Using the same haz-mat example, an IC with limited resources may only be able to appoint a Haz-Mat Group Supervisor to deal with control, containment, and decontamination. Given greater resources, the IC might appoint a supervisor for a Control Group, one for the Containment Group, and another for the Decontamination Group.

A trap some ICs fall into is that of trying to fill slots within the ICS structure while the building burns down. This can be caused either because the IC is so busy creating subordinate positions that no one is left to fight the fire, or because the IC is so busy managing the command structure that nobody is managing the incident.

Fires are not easily impressed by organizational charts but are most often impacted by fire fighters working their buns off in a well-coordinated attack. The Incident Command System is a management tool which allows the IC to better manage and coordinate the efforts of those fire fighters and the other available resources. Positions within ICS should only be filled when they will assist the IC in meeting the incident goals and objectives and not filled just to build a better organizational chart. The fire can tell the difference.

The benefits of using ICS to apply sound management principles are many:

* It works at any type of emergency no matter how large, small or complex;

* It provides for unity of command--one person in charge with clear line of authority, responsibility and accountability;

* Clear lines of communication are established;

* Freelance fire fighting is eliminated or minimized;

* Incidents involving multiple agencies or jurisdictions can be dealt with through improved coordination and communication provided by a common emergency management system;

* The system can be expanded in a modular fashion as the incident expands or as additional resources become available;

* More effective use of resources;

* Personnel safety can be enhanced.

From a personal standpoint, the "pucker factor" can be reduced allowing you to be a better manager — rather than dragging the seat cushion from your vehicle behind you throughout the incident!

32

# THE ICS TOOLBOX

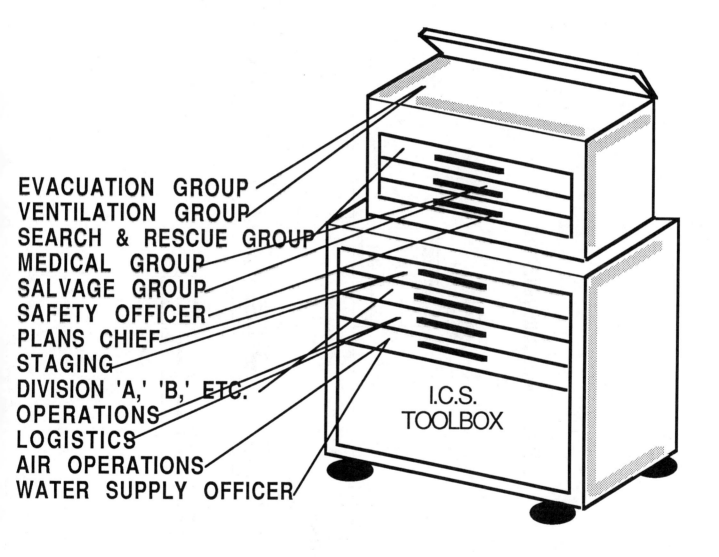

EVACUATION GROUP
VENTILATION GROUP
SEARCH & RESCUE GROUP
MEDICAL GROUP
SALVAGE GROUP
SAFETY OFFICER
PLANS CHIEF
STAGING
DIVISION 'A,' 'B,' ETC.
OPERATIONS
LOGISTICS
AIR OPERATIONS
WATER SUPPLY OFFICER

I.C.S.
TOOLBOX

## USE ONLY THOSE TOOLS WHICH ARE NEEDED
## (LEAVE THE OTHERS IN THE BOX)

# The IC Organizational Chart

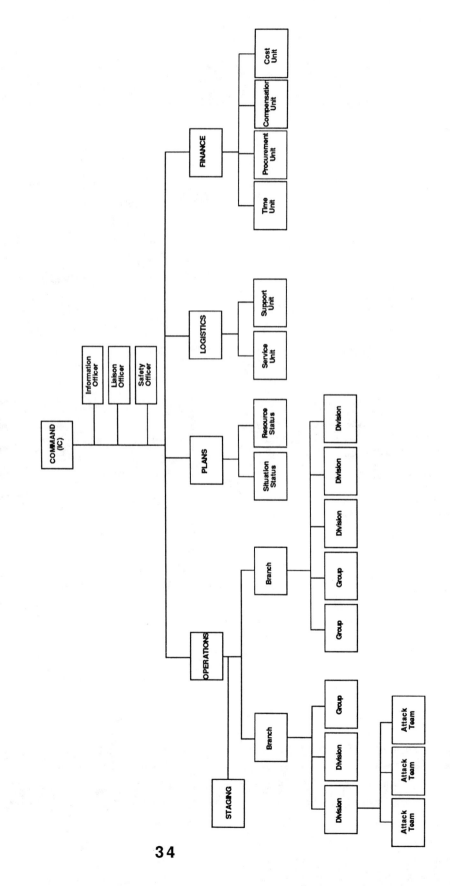

# A GUIDE FOR SUCCESSFUL SCENE MANAGEMENT

**ON-SCENE REPORT**

WHAT DO I HAVE?
* Residential
  - One-story
  - Two-story
  - Mobile home
  - Garage
* Commercial
  - Common Attic
  - Warehouse
  - Office
  - Center Hall
  - Center Core
* SIZE OF STRUCTURE
* TYPE OF CONSTRUCTION
* AMOUNT AND COLOR OF SMOKE AND FLAME
* EVACUATION OR RESCUE NEEDS

WHAT AM I DOING?
* INTERIOR OR EXTERIOR ATTACK
  - Size of Lines
  - From What Access Point In (e.g., Front Door)
* SEARCH AND RESCUE
* VENTILATION
* PROTECTING EXPOSURES
* LAYING OWN SUPPLY LINES
* MEETING INFORMANT

WHAT DO I NEED?
* SUPPLY LINE
* BACK-UP LINE
* PRIMARY/SECONDARY SEARCH
* VENTILATION
* FORCIBLE ENTRY
* BUILDING LADDERED
* UTILITIES

WHO IS IN COMMAND?
* IT IS IMPERATIVE THAT AN INCIDENT COMMANDER BE DESIGNATED

- Relay who is IC to all responding units
- When possible, pass command when making an interior attack

**INCIDENT SIZE UP SHOULD ADDRESS:**
* LIFE SAFETY
* INCIDENT STABLIZATION
* PROPERTY CONSERVATION

RESCUE:
* Occupancy Type and Use
* Number of Possible Occupants
* Time of Day/Week
* Primary and Secondary Search
* Specialized Rescue
* Evaluate Body Recovery vs. Rescue Potential

EVACUATION:
* Exposures
* Downhill/Downwind in the Event of a Haz-mat Incident
* Police Department Assistance

VENTILATION:
* Vertical
* Horizontal
* Positive Pressure vs. Natural
* Location and Size of Roof Cuts
* Wind Direction
* Building Configurations
* HVAC Assessment
* TImely and Coordinated with Fire Attack

ATTACK:
* Personally View as Many Sides of the Building as Possible
* Exposure Protection
* Primary and Secondary Search
  - Timely
  - Adequate Resource Assigned

35

- Completion of Search
  Relayed to IC
* Apparatus Spotted Appropriately
  - Don't Block Other Units
  - Have a Way Out
  - Don't Gang Up at the
    Front Door
* Fire Attack
  - Attack from the
    Unburned Interior Side
  - Back Up
  - GPM vs. BTUs
  - Correct Size and
    Arrangement of Lines
  - Protect Interior Access
    and Escape Routes
  - Protect Search Crews
  - Write Off Property
    Already Lost
  - Confine Fire
  - Check for Extention
  - Coordinate with Proper
    Ventilation
* Water Supply
  - Adequate Volume
    Available
  - Adequate Personnel
    and Equipment Available
  - Large Diameter Supply
    Lines
  - Relay Pumping
  - Drafting
  - Tanker Shuttle

SALVAGE:
  * Salvage assessment
  * Save the irreplaceable,
    high ticket items
  * Remove
  * Cover
  * Ventilate

UTILIZATION OF BUILT-IN SYSTEMS:
  * STANDPIPES
  * SPRINKLERS
  * COMMUNICATION AND
    CONTROL SYSTEMS
  * HVAC
  * ELEVATORS

UTILITIES:
  * ELECTRICAL SHUT OFF

* GAS SHUT OFF
* APPROPRIATE UTILITY
  COMPANY NOTIFIED

SAFETY:
  * RECOGNITION OF HAZARDS
    - Collapse
    - Explosion
    - Backdraft
    - Flashover
    - Hazardous Materials
    - Overhead Electrical
      Lines
  * SAFETY OFFICER
  * NO FREELANCE CREWS
  * COORDINATED USE OF
    INTERIOR/EXTERIOR LINES
  * BUDDY SYSTEM (NO
    SPLITTING OF WORKING TEAMS)
  * CORRECT USE OF
    "EMERGENCY TRAFFIC"

SCENE MANAGEMENT:
  * COMMUNICATIONS:
    - Clear
    - Concise
    - Use Proper Frequencies
    - Set Confirmation for Directives
      Given (e.g., "E-2 Copies, Lay in a
      Supply Line")

  * USE ELEMENTS OF THE INCIDENT
    COMMAND SYSTEM:
    - Appropriately
    - Use Only What You Actually
      Need (Tool Box)
    - Maintain a Reasonable Span of
      Control
    - Anticipate Need for Additional
      Equipment, Personnel
    - Plan Ahead; Have a Plan 'B'
    - Change Plan as Conditions
      Change
    - Do Not Keep Personnel in
      Untennable Conditions
    - Evaluate Need for Specialized
      Equipment, Supplies, and
      Technical Advice
    - Maximize Use of Personnel and
      Equipment

*Format for this guide courtesy of Gus Sitas, company officer, Poudre Fire Authority, Fort Collins, Colorado*

# Successful Scene Management
## * * STUDENT ACTIVITY * *

1. List the three steps to successful incident management:

    1) *Think*

    2) *Plan*

    3) *Act*

2. What does GYST stand for?

    *Get your self Together*

3. When doing a size-up, the company officer must address three incident priorities. List them in order of importance:

    1) *Life Safety*

    2) *Incident Stabilization*

    3) *Property Conservation*

4. What is size-up?

    *Pg 24*

5. What does REVAS mean?

    *Rescue, Evacuation Ventilation Attack + Salvage*

6. The first arriving officer should communicate to other incoming units a complete arrival report. This report should include four topic areas. List them:

1) what do I have

2) what am I doing

3) what's needed

4) who's in command.

7. A good, effective plan addresses two key questions. They are:

1) what has to be done

2) How's it going to be done

8. What was the Incident Command System developed?

Out of Firescope

9. What does NIMS stand for?

National Incident mgt System
            Interagency

10. The structure of ICS is divided into five functional areas. These areas are:

1) Planning

2) Logistics

3) Command

4) Finance

5) Operation

11. The Command Staff positions are:

1) S.O.

2) PIO

3) Liaison

12. Explain the Operation's Chief's role in the ICS system:

Responsible for Tactics + Operation control.

13. Branch Directors, when activated, report to the:

Ops Chief

14. What is Staging, and how is it used?

Un-assigned resources report for a back-up or until need for assignment. pg. 30

15. What is Planning responsible for?

Gathering + assimilation of Info. pg 30

16. What is Logistics responsible for?

Facilities / Services Needed pg 30

17. What is Finance responsible for?

All aspects of the incident pg 31

39

18. You are the Incident Commander on a structure fire that involves an industrial complex storing hazardous materials. Resources on the scene are four engines, two trucks, a squad unit, a Haz-mat unit, two medic units and three divisional officers. Diagram an IC organizational chart which could be used on this incident.

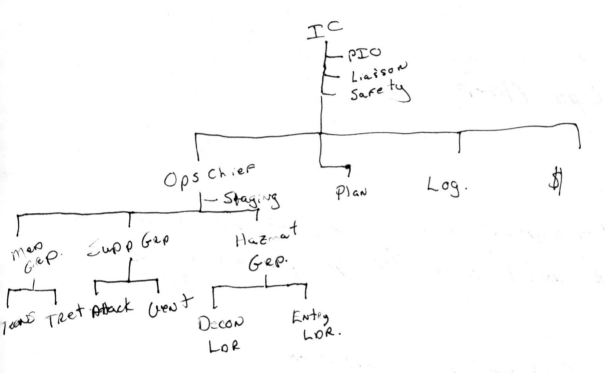

# MODULE THREE

## FIREGROUND VENTILATION TECHNIQUES

# VIDEO NOTES

# FIREGROUND VENTILATION TECHNIQUES

## Introduction

*Ventilation, or smoke removal, is the process of removing products of combustion from a fire area to assist fire fighting operations.* Used properly, ventilation becomes an integral part of efficient rescue, fire control, salvage and overhaul operations. Smoke is a by-product of every fire and must be dealt with quickly and efficiently if objectives of fire fighting operations are to be accomplished. Heavy concentrations of smoke hinder firefighters in the performance of their duties by reducing visibility. In addition, today's modern materials generate products of combustion that present a very real threat to the safety and welfare of all personnel in an affected area.

Smoke removal begins with the arrival of the first company and continues until all smoke has been removed. Excessive amounts of smoke contribute to fire loss. The longer smoke is allowed to remain in a structure, the more extensive the loss becomes.

Modern technology requires the fire service to reassess the importance ventilation plays in effective fire attack. Since the mid-twentieth century, the use of plastic and related materials has experienced phenomenal growth. As a result, fuel loads, BTUs and toxic gases found in today's structure fires are dramatically increased. As in years past, effective ventilation is a must for the saving of lives, suppression of fire and reduction of damage to the property involved.

## The Advantages of Ventilation

As fire fighters, our purpose is to prevent and/or minimize the threat to life and property as a result of fire. To accomplish this, the firefighter is required to perform rescue operations and fire extinguishment while minimizing the damage caused by the fire and subsequent fire fighting operations. Ventilation, if used appropriately, can have a tremendous impact on every aspect of fireground activity. No function on the fireground is as neglected or as misunderstood as ventilation. <u>Failure to ventilate, premature ventilation, or improper ventilation are major causes of large-loss fires and increased fire fighter injury.</u> Performed properly, ventilation can enhance the fireground situation. For example:

1. <u>Rescue operations</u> are expedited as the atmosphere within a structure is made more tenable by the release of heat and toxic gases. This quickens the search and rescue operations and provides fresh air for the occupants of the building, reducing the danger of asphyxiation.
2. <u>Fire attack</u> is made easier by proper ventilation as the fire can be found more rapidly and extinguished.
3. <u>Reduction in property damage</u> is a direct result of proper ventilation: a) Water damage is reduced through rapid extinguishment; b) Salvage can be initiated sooner; and c) Smoke damages are reduced.
4. <u>Thermal stratification</u> is minimized, which reduces the smoke and heat fire fighters must endure while making interior attack. In addition, proper ventilation will decrease the horizontal spread of fire, reducing thermal stratification and mushrooming of smoke and fire gases.
5. <u>Backdraft</u>, or the potential for backdraft, can be substantially reduced when a well-placed ventilation hole is cut allowing gases to safely escape.

In the Fire Attack series, we will study the importance of ventilation as a primary attack tool; however, a good fire officer must assess the use and importance of ventilation based on the conditions present at each fire incident:
* Is there a need for ventilation?
* Where is ventilation needed?
* What type of ventilation will be most beneficial?
* What visible smoke conditions exist?

* What type of building is involved?
* What are the life hazards?
* Where is the location and what is the extent of the fire?

Before ventilating a building, a fire officer should have assessed these factors prior to ordering ventilation to begin. Always remember: <u>The impact ventilation can have upon a fire can be very severe.</u> As a fireground participant, make sure you have the resources available for fire control if the fire should intensify or if exposure protection is needed as a result of ventilation operations.

## Ventilation Techniques

There are three principal methods to ventilate a building charged with smoke.
1. Horizontal
2. Vertical
3. Forced

**Horizontal Ventilation:** *Horizontal ventilation is performed by opening windows and doors to allow air currents to relieve the structure of smoke and gases.* Remember: Open the windows on the leeward side first, and then open the windward side. Structures in which horizontal ventilation can be effective are:
- Residential buildings
- Buildings with large window openings
- Unsupported open space structures, such as garages, etc.

**Vertical Ventilation:** *Vertical ventilation is performed by opening the roof area through natural openings (sky lights, scuttle holes, vents) or by emergency openings made by fire fighting personnel.* Vertical ventilation allows the natural convection of the heated gases to rise through the vertical opening, thus improving the atmospheric conditions within the involved structure. Vertical ventilation will not be the solution to all ventilation problems you will face and may be impractical in some of the structures to which you will respond.

**Forced Ventilation:** *Forced ventilation is accomplished by the use of smoke ejectors, fans, fog streams, or some internal air evacuation system.* The use of forced ventilation provides several advantages.

* More positive control
* Supplements natural ventilation methods
* Facilitates the removal of contaminants
* Reduces smoke damage

However, forced ventilation can:
* Increase the spread of fire both horizontally and vertically
* Be dependent upon an outside power source
* Requires special equipment
* Requires special knowledge

Historically and traditionally, most fire fighters have placed smoke ejectors in windows or doorways in an attempt to suck or "eject" smoke from the building.

Ejecting smoke can present several problems:

1. Fire fighters must be exposed to the smoke-filled environment to set up the smoke ejectors in doorways, windows, or other exit openings.
2. Smoke ejectors have a tendency to become fouled by sucking up any loose fire debris in the area, such as curtains, and propelling it through the blades, creating additional safety problems.
3. Highly portable internal combustion powered smoke ejectors do not run properly in smoke-filled, oxygen deficient atmospheres.
4. The sucking of smoke, heat, and the products of combustion through an ejector creates cleaning and maintenance problems.
5. Placement of smoke ejectors in doorways creates an additional safety hazard by blocking normal ingress and egress of fire fighters.
6. Noise from the smoke ejectors adds to the confusion on the fireground.
7. Ejecting smoke does not take optimum benefit from the physical laws that apply to the creation of pressure differential.

## Positive Pressure Ventiliation

Because of the aforementioned problems, the Los Angeles City Fire Department has experimented over the years with smoke ejectors, both on a trial and error

**44**

basis, as well as with carefully controlled experiments. The findings from these experiments have led to a system of forced ventilation called "Positive Pressure Ventilation." As remarkable as it may seem, the optimum method of removing smoke from buildings or vessels using forced ventilation turned out to be a system of creating pressure differentials by "blowing" into the building or vessel rather than trying to suck or "eject" the smoke. Thus, the term *blowers* was invented.

By directing blowers inward, pressure can be created inside a building or vessel that is higher than that of the outside environment. As long as the pressure is higher inside the building, the smoke within the structure will have no choice but to seek an outlet to a lower pressure zone through openings controlled by fire fighters.

The advantages of positive pressure ventilation include:

#5

1. Fire fighters can set up forced ventilation procedures without entering a smoke-filled environment.
2. A greater quantity of smoke and heat can be removed from the structure at a more efficient rate.
3. The velocity of air currents within the building is kept to a minimum. Contents and smoldering debris are hardly disturbed, if at all. Yet, the total exchange of air within the building is greater than ejecting smoke from within the

building to the outside.
4. Placement of smoke ejectors does not interfere with ingress or egress.
5. Internal combustion powered equipment operates more efficiently in the clean, oxygen-rich air.
6. Cleaning and maintenance of equipment is greatly reduced.
7. When equipment is placed outside the building, noise levels are reduced within the structure.
8. This system is applicable to all types of structures and is particularly effective at removing smoke from large and/or high-ceiling areas where attempts to suck or eject smoke are ineffective.
9. Heat and smoke may be directed away from unburned areas or paths of exit.

As an example, let's consider a fire in a one-story, single-family dwelling with smoke spread throughout the building. Once the fire is extinguished, the smoke can be removed by using simple positive pressure ventilation techniques.

The first step is to set up a blower on the windward side of the building, approximately five to twelve feet from a door or a window. It is very important to aim the pressure cone from the blower so that it covers the entire area of the door or window. If the pressure cone only partially covers the entry point, air will escape or leak around the area not covered.

45

After the building is pressurized so that the interior pressure is above that of the outside atmosphere, the most efficient application will require closing doors within the building and pressurizing one room at a time until the smoke is cleared. It is important to keep the exit opening from being larger than the entry opening, or the positive pressure will be lost and it will take longer to remove the smoke. An exit opening approximately three-fourths the size of the entry opening will generally provide optimum smoke removal.

Forced ventilation using positive pressure is more a volume operation than a velocity operation. By closing doors within the structure and pressurizing one room or area at a time, the process of removing the smoke is speeded up because of the increased velocity of air movement. Placing additional equipment at the entry point also speeds up the process. If none of the doors inside the structure were opened and closed systematically, the process would still work; but it would take substantially more time.

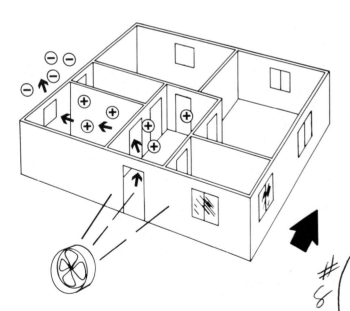

Positive pressure ventilation works equally well in above-ground fire fighting operations. The same principles apply, but greater coordination is generally required to control interior fire doors so that positive pressure is directed to the appropriate floor. Note that positive pressure is applied to the building at ground

level through the use of one or more blowers. The positive pressure is then directed throughout the building by opening and closing doors until the building is totally cleared of smoke through any opening selected by fire fighters.

When using positive pressure to remove smoke from multiple floors of a building, it is generally best to apply the positive pressure at the lowest point. Smoke can then be systematically removed one floor at a time, starting with the lowest floor.

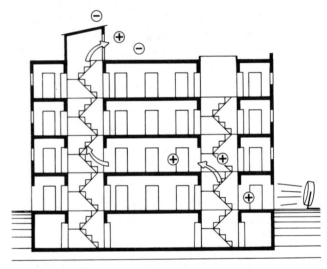

This system also works well in high-rise buildings and can be used either to assist in cross ventilation of fire floors, or to direct smoke up a stairshaft to a rooftop opening. Positive pressure ventilation tests in high-rise buildings using multiple blowers at street level have provided positive pressure through a closed stairshaft to the rooftop of twenty-story buildings in less than thirty seconds!

The main problem that will be encountered when using positive pressure ventilation in above-ground operations is the coordination of opening and closing doors in the stairshaft used to pressurize the building. Curious tenants may stand with the door to the stairshaft or their room open. This redirects the positive pressure away from the fire floor. Placing one person in charge of the pressurizing process, using portable radios, and/or having fire fighters patrol the stairshaft and hallways will be helpful in controlling the operation. The main points to remember when using

**46**

positive pressure ventilation are:

1. Take advantage of existing wind conditions.
2. Make certain that the air cone from the blower covers the entire entry opening.
3. Do not allow the exit opening to become larger than the entry opening, or the efficiency of the operation will be greatly reduced.
4. Positive pressure ventilation is more of a volume operation than a velocity operation. To speed up the process, reduce the size of the area being pressurized by systematically opening and closing doors or by increasing the number or size of blowers in use.
5. Positive pressure can be applied at several entry points to channel heat and smoke away from unburned areas or paths of exit.
6. Positive pressure ventilation uses the simplest of principles. Until the procedure is understood by all personnel on the fireground, problems may occur with the blowers being repositioned without considering the impact on the overall operation.
   <u>Best results will be achieved by placing responsibility for ventilation with one person.</u>

47

# Fireground Ventilation Techniques
## **STUDENT ACTIVITY**

1. What is ventilation?

*Pg 43*

Removing products of combustion
from a fire area to assist
fire fighting ops

2. List four advantages proper ventilation can have on fire-ground activities:

*Pg 43*

1) Rescue Ops are Expedited

2) Fire Attack is made easier

3) Reduction in Property Damage

4) Thermal stratification is minimized

5) Backdraft potential reduced

3. A good fire officer must assess each fire to determine if ventilation will be useful. List four of the factors which should be reviewed before ventilating a building:

*Pg 43*

1) Is there a need?

2) Where is ventilation needed

3) What type of ventilation will be most beneficial

4) What visable Smoke conditions exist.

4. There are three principal methods of ventilation.  List and briefly explain each:

*Pg 44*   1) *Vertical ventilation (Opening Roof Area*

2) *Forced  P.P.V.*

3) *Horizontal*

5. What are five advantages of positive pressure ventilation?

1)

2)

*Pg  45*

3)

4)

5)

6. Positive pressure ventilation is more a _____*Volume*_____
operation than a
_____*Velocity*_____ operation.

7. When using positive pressure to remove smoke from multiple floors of a building, it generally best to apply the positive pressure where?

*At the lowest point  pg 46*

8. The main problem in using positive pressure ventilation in above-ground operations is:

Coordinating opening and closing
of Doors
Pg 46

9. _____True ___✓___False. Ventilation should never be considered as a primary fire attack tool.

10. Ventilation, even if done properly, can have a severe impact on the overall fireground operation. As a fire fighter, company officer, or IC you should make sure you have "what" available and "why"?

11. You have responded to a one-room fire in a single family residence. You have been assigned to ventilate the structure. Outline what your ventilation assessment would include and anticipate what ventilation techniques will be used.

1. Size up
2. How ~~Leoter~~ Leavy involved
P.P.U. or Verticle.

50

# MODULE FOUR

## RESIDENTIAL FIRE ATTACK

# VIDEO NOTES

_____

_____

_____

_____

_____

_____

_____

_____

_____

_____

_____

_____

_____

_____

_____

_____

_____

_____

_____

_____

_____

_____

# RESIDENTIAL FIRE ATTACK

## Introduction

The United States Fire Service responded to 2,371,000 fires in 1985; 72% occurred in residential properties. Fires in the home accounted for 4,885 civilian deaths; which accounts for 79% of all fire deaths during that year. In addition, 69% of all civilian injuries occurred in residential properties.

Every community has the typical type of occupancies we will cover in this section:

- The one-story house
- The two-story house
- Attached garages
- Alley fires

Although residential fires are the most common responded to by American Fire Service personnel, each problem will demand its own solution; and each solution may be vastly different. Success or failure on the fireground is largely dependent upon that first-in company's ability to assess the overall situation, decide what action is to be taken, and to set the plan into action. In Module Four, we will review many of the common problems encountered in residential fire attack and how they can be avoided or overcome by applying some basic fireground techniques.

## The One-Story House

**SCENARIO:** A one-story house with the bedroom well-involved and spreading into the hallway and/or adjacent bedroom; or one-story house with the living room well-involved, spreading into hallway and/or adjoining rooms.

**STRATEGY:** The ideal strategy in fires of this type is to fight the fire from the <u>uninvolved</u> side and push it back into the involved area.

If at all possible, vertical ventilation should be performed as soon as possible. This will:
*Stop the horizontal spread of the fire
*Lower temperature and toxic atmosphere

inside the dwelling
*Increase visibility
*Allow for venting of steam from extinguishment
*Create workable, tenable atmosphere for fire fighters following knockdown

Rescue considerations:
*Nighttime is most severe as there is a greater probability of occupants being at home, asleep, and in need of rescue
*Regardless of time of day, searches will have to be made:
*Primary search* — *A quick thorough search as conditions allow during the initial fireground operation*
*Secondary search* — *Rescue functions that follow lengthy fire control activities will be regarded as representing secondary search.*

Ask yourself: Why do we have a need for rescue? And what is causing it?
*Fire
*Smoke conditions
*Occupant's condition
*Building condition

The fire is the problem!!!
The sooner we can knock it down with a direct attack on the seat of the fire, the sooner we can eliminate the problem that is endangering the occupants.
*Try to work from uninvolved into the involved
*Although not always possible, attacking from the involved side is a calculated risk and should be carefully considered

What size hose line should be used?
We are talking about structural fire fighting. Anything less than a 1 1/2-inch line is too small.
*GPM versus BTU

Booster lines, hose reels, etc., are for incidental fires. The use of these types of lines on a structure is the best way to slowly burn a house down. It is also a dangerous practice and should be eliminated. The use of inappropriately sized hand lines will:

*Teach you to fight fires while walking and crawling backwards
*Increase the chances of your fire fighters suffering severe burns from flashover
*Give your department plenty of ammunition for telling war stories on how we lost another one
*Provide good news footage of a house burning to ground

How many hoselines should be utilized?
   *If at all possible, two hose lines to the seat of the fire
   *That backup hoseline could save your life if the unexpected should happen:
      -- Broken hose line
      -- Kinked hose
      -- Clogged nozzle
      -- Flashover
      -- Backdraft

The bulk of the fire is knocked down.  Now what?
   * Congratulate your Captain?
   *Congratulate your Chief?
   *Congratulate your fellow fire fighters

   NOT YET!!

Which way will heat and fire travel?
   * Into the attic
   * Into walls
   *Through pipe chases

Be sure and check the attic as soon as possible.  If there are any indications of fire in the attic or if you cannot find the scuttle hole, pull the ceiling.  This action may very well save the entire structure.

Where should you pull the ceiling?
   *Get ahead of the fire and pull the ceiling between the seat of the fire and its direction of travel.

If it is a marginal situation, and you are not sure you have fire in the attic and you cannot find the scuttle hole,
   *Pull ceiling directly over the seat of the fire
   *Chances are the drywall is ruined anyway

How big a hole should you pull?

*If there is any indication of fire in the attic whatsoever, pull a hole that is big enough so you can place a line in service into the attic.

*The most common mistake in pulling ceilings is not pulling enough ceiling fast enough, which allows the fire to gain control of the attic, the incident, and you!!

A small access hole in the ceiling will:
   *Keep the hose stream from hitting fire
   *Increase water damage to the structure
   *Assist you in burning the house down

What type of tools will be effective in pulling ceilings?
   *Pike pole
   *Extension or step ladder
   *Plaster hook

Opening walls:
   *Feel for hot spots
   *Use pick-headed ax to open walls
   *When in doubt, open wall and then a little more
   *Fire could have traveled up the wall, into the attic.

**STRATEGY AND TACTICS**
Let's review our fire attack on the one-story house.

Copyright© 1987 Emergency Resource Inc.

**Rescue/Evacuation:** In this type of occupancy, the rescue problem is the prime objective. Nighttime fires indicate a greater probability of occupants in need of rescue.

      *Primary search
      *Secondary search

**Ventilation:** Ventilation strategy will be to utilize vertical ventilation, if at all possible. This will

      *assist in controlling the horizontal spread.
      *reduce the toxic atmosphere inside the dwelling.
      *create a workable environment for fire personnel.
      *speed extinguishment and rescue operations.

**Attack the Fire:**
      *Attack the fire from the uninvolved side and push it back to the involved areas.
      *Minimum 1 1/2-inch hoseline
      *What is your strategy?! The strategy is to position hand lines to protect uninvolved portions of the structure and interior exit stairways.
      *A quick, aggressive interior attack on the seat of the fire, in coordination with proper vertical ventilation, and a good primary search will greatly reduce the lives lost and property damage sustained in this type of occupancy.

**Salvage:** A quick aggressive interior attack from the uninvolved side is the best way to reduce fire loss. Depending on your resources, salvage work should begin as soon as possible:

      *Salvage covers
      *Floor runners
      *Rolled plastic/visquine
      *Pressurize the building

# Single-Family Residence

## Fire Problem #4-1

<u>DISPATCH INFORMATION</u>: VIDEO FOOTAGE

You are dispatched to a reported structure fire in a single-family residence. The home is a one-story, three-bedroom, ranch style house with an attached two-car garage. The house is built of standard wood-frame construction with some exterior brick veneer. The roof is made of typical wood truss construction with asphalt shingle overlay.

The time of alarm is 2:00 a.m. The temperature is 60° F., and the winds are from the south at 5 M.P.H.

<u>ARRIVAL INFORMATION</u>: FIRE SLIDE

Upon arrival, you discover moderate smoke coming from the rear of the house. No flames are visible at this time. The owner of the house meets you at the engine and states that the house is fully occupied and that he saw heavy smoke and flames coming from his family room as he exited the home.

You are responding with your department's first alarm assignment and your engine company is first on the scene.

"LET'S                    FIGHT                    THIS                    FIRE"

57

58

## ONE-STORY RESIDENTIAL

### Figure 4-1

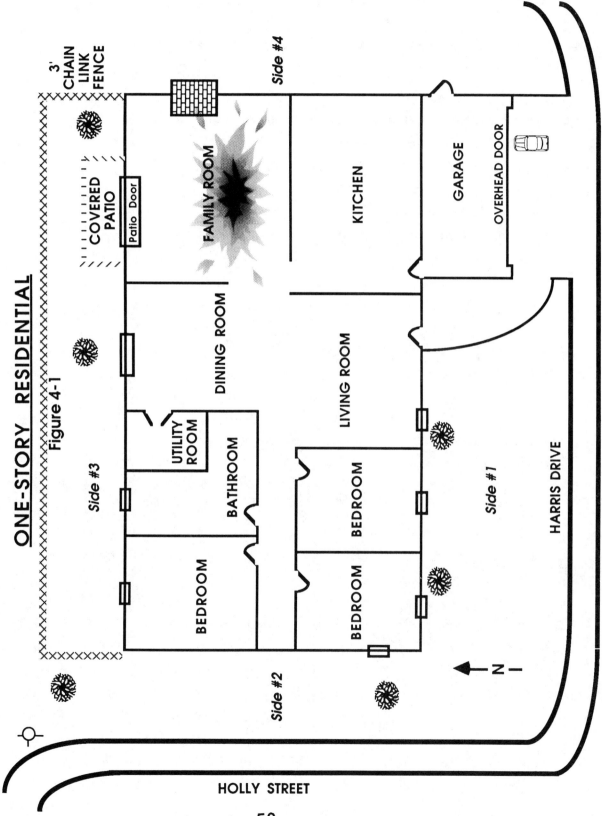

## * * STUDENT ACTIVITY * *
### Fire Problem #4-1

1. Carefully study the floor plan and fire photo for fire problem 4-1 and read the dispatch information.

2. As first officer on the scene, write a brief narrative of your arrival report:

3. Using <u>REVAS</u>, what were your incident priorities and how were they addressed?

RESCUE:

EVACUATION:

VENTILATION:




ATTACK:




SALVAGE:




4. On the floor plan draw the location of:

       1) Responding apparatus
       2) Fire attack hose lines
       3) Water supply
       4) Location and method of ventilation


5. How would you manage this incident? Draw an incident command structure that you would use on this problem.

# TheTwo-Story House

Most two-story homes are designed with the bedrooms upstairs and the kitchen and living quarters downstairs. Obviously, then,we are going to encounter fires on the first floor, second floor, and/or both.

The time of day is critical for a house fire.
* Nighttime: Life hazard severe
* Daytime: Life hazard lessens

**SCENARIO I:** A two-story house with fire on first floor kitchen and living room well-involved.

**STRATEGY:** The ideal strategy here is to stop the vertical spread to the second floor. Unfortunately, the amount of heat and smoke generated with the kitchen and living room well-involved will have filled the second floor unless bedroom doors are closed. Rarely will two-story houses have fire doors at the top of the stair separating floors.

**Rescue/Evacuation:** If the fire is at night, the rescue problem is serious. As indicated previously, nighttime fires indicate a greater probability of occupants in need of rescue.
*Primary search
*Secondary search

**Ventilation:** A fast attack coupled with proper ventilation will probably save the most lives and result in the lowest property loss.

The objectives will be to:
*Stop vertical spread
*Stop horizontal spread
*Lower temperature inside dwelling
*Increase visibility
*Allow for venting of steam from extinguishment
*Create workable, tenable atmosphere for fire fighters following knockdown

Where do you start?
*Start at the top and work down
* Open up over stairway by cutting the roof and using vertical ventilation
*Open windows on second floor
* Open windows on first floor

**Attack the Fire:** With a good fire going on the first floor, where do you start the attack?
*Above the fire to stop the vertical spread?
*Direct attack on the seat of the fire on first floor? The odds are in your favor to make a direct attack on the seat of the fire on the first floor.
*Try to protect stairshaft
*Attack fire from uninvolved toward the involved side
*Second hoseline above the fire
*Stop vertical spread

Third hoseline (if needed) backup the first hoseline. What size hoselines?
* Remember, nothing smaller than 1 1/2-inch lines for structure fire fighting
*GPM vs. BTU

Salvage: Start salvage as soon as possible
*Cover furniture to protect it from smoke, water, and steam
*Keep doors closed on upper floors to keep out smoke

*Salvage covers
*Floor runner
*Plastic

**SCENARIO II:** Two-story house with fire on the second floor. Two bedrooms well-involved spreading into hallway. Using REVAS:

**Rescue/Evacuation:** If the fire is at night, the rescue problem is serious.
    *Primary search
    *Secondary search

**Ventilation:** An aggressive attack coupled with proper ventilation will probably save the most lives and result in the lowest property loss.

The objectives will be to:
    *Stop vertical spread
    *Stop horizontal spread
    *Lower temperature inside dwelling

*Increase visibility
*Allow for venting of steam from extinguishment
*Create workable, tenable atmosphere for fire fighters following knockdown

Where do you start?
    *Open the roof as close to the seat of fire as can be done safely.
    *When control of the fire is accomplished, positive pressure ventilation will provide the best method of smoke removal.

**Attack the Fire:** Direct attack on the seat of the fire:
    *Attack from <u>uninvolved</u> into the <u>involved</u> side
    *Back up first hoseline with a second hose line
    *Size of the hose line should be 1-1/2-inch or larger for structure fire fighting

— Pull the ceilings:
    *This is a high priority
    *Check for vertical extension
    *Bring in small step ladder to gain access to attic
    *Pull ceiling between fire and direction of spread

**Salvage:** With a good fire going on the second floor, it is going to take considerable GPM to knockdown the BTUs.

Remember: Water runs downhill and plumbers get paid on Friday. Designate personnel to begin salvage on the first floor as soon as possible.

Also remember:
    *Approximate location of fire above you
    *Place furniture in center of room and cover
    *Salvage covers
    *Floor runners
    *Rolled plastic
    *Construct water chutes to direct water out of structure
    *Pressurize the building

**SCENARIO III:** A two-story house with fire has spread from the first floor to the second floor. Using REVAS:

**Rescue/Evacuation:** If the fire is at night, the rescue problem is serious
    *Primary search
    *Secondary search

**Attack the Fire:** Ventilation coupled with a fast attack on the fire will probably save the most lives and result in the lowest property loss.

Work your way up
    First hoseline to the first floor
        *Attack from the <u>uninvolved</u> side to
          the <u>involved</u> side
    Second hoseline above the fire
        *<u>Uninvolved</u> to <u>involved</u>
    Third hoseline
        *Backup on first floor
    Fourth hoseline
        *Backup on second floor
    Pull ceilings
        *High priority
        *Check for vertical extension
        *Step ladder for attic access
        *Pull ceiling between fire and direction
         of travel

**Salvage:** Protect those areas not affected by the extensive fire. Prepare for water from above:
    *Place furnishings in center of room and cover
    *Salvage covers
    *Floor runner
    *Plastic
    *Construct water chutes to direct water out of
     structure

# The Attached Garage

**SCENARIO:** A single family dwelling with an attached garage. The garage is well-involved in fire upon arrival of the company. The first-in officer isn't sure whether the fire has already spread to the house; but if it hasn't, it will spread to the uninvolved areas very quickly.

**STRATEGY:** Where does the first hoseline go?
    *Inside the structure to stay the spread?
    *Attack the main bulk of the fire in the garage?
    *Pull back and protect the house exposed
     next door?

Play the percentages; take the best odds.
    *Chances are that by making a quick attack on
     the main bulk of the fire, the garage, and
     knocking this fire down, we will eliminate the
     problem that is causing the fire to spread into
     the dwelling.
    *Yes, the attack on the garage may push fire
     into the dwelling; but, by knocking down the
     main source of heat, we have a better chance
     of saving more of the house.
    *With the main bulk of the fire knocked down,
     we must then move quickly to check for
     extension into the house. This is an ideal
     assignment for the second company which
     can place a second line into service in the
     house and check for possible extension.

What could go wrong with this strategy?
    *The most common argument will be that you
     should get inside the house and protect it
     from the fire spreading from the garage; then
     assign the well- involved garage to the
     second company.

Will this work?
    *It might! But the odds are that unless your
     second company is on the scene within a

**64**

reasonable time frame, the garage fire will grow in intensity and eventually spread to the dwelling at multiple locations, mainly through the attic.

Once the main fire is knocked down, you will be involved in extensive mop-up operations with hidden wall and attic fires. Chances are also great that the house will suffer severe smoke damage.

**ARGUMENT:** The garage is protected with one-hour plaster or drywall. Why worry? We have one hour before the fire will spread to the house. DON'T COUNT ON IT!!

*Garages can have an extremely heavy fire load.
- Gasoline          - Motorcycles
- Paint             - Miscellaneous storage
- Thinner           - Etc.
- Autos

Premature failure of this fire barrier and extension is common due to the heavy fire loads and the openness of the structure; i.e., garage doors, unprotected rafters.
  *Holes in the walls or ceilings from installing and moving shelves and fixtures are not that uncommon; this contributes to rapid fire spread.
  *Remember . . . if at all possible, knock down the main source of heat as soon as possible.
  *Get rid of the source of your problem, which is the main bulk of the fire.

Once the main bulk of the fire is knocked down, quickly check for horizontal and vertical extension into the structure:
  *Attic
  *Walls
  *Any possible concealed spaces

What additional problems exist if the house is two-story and portions of the house are built over the garage?
  *Life hazard
  *More likelihood of extension
  *Higher probability of structural collapse

How does this change your strategy?
  *Basically the strategy remains the same — remove the source that is causing the problem.

*Hit the main fire hard and fast!!
*Remember: A simultaneous primary search will be needed immediately.
*Position hose lines above the fire to stop vertical spread.

There is no right or wrong way to handle this type of fire. It requires a judgment call. Either you go for protecting the house and hope that a second line or company will knock down the main bulk of the fire, or you eliminate the source of the problem by a fast hard-hitting attack on the seat of the fire, followed up by quickly checking for horizontal and vertical spread.

Play the percentages!! Keep the odds in your favor!!

Let us take another look using REVAS:

**Rescue/Evacuation:** Life hazard in attached garages is minimal, unless
  *Someone was in the garage at the time of the fire
  *The garage is built under a portion of the house
  *An explosion or flash fire has occurred

Remember . . . just because it is a garage fire, <u>NEVER</u> discount doing a thorough primary search.

**Ventilation:** The openness of the typical garage lends itself to positive pressure ventilation. Where do you start?

> *Set 2 - 3 smoke ejectors facing the overhead garage door approximately 10 - 12 feet from the doorway.
> *Open back door or window to garage and ventilate.
> *If no back door exists, you may continue positive pressure if a roof hole has been cut.
> *Evacuate the smoke from the garage by drawing or sucking the contaminates from the area.

**Attack the Fire:** Two strategies for this type of fire exist:

> 1) Make a quick attack on the main bulk of the fire.
> 2) Attack from the uninvolved side (usually the house portion) and contain the fire in the garage area

Whichever attack is utilized, it is imperative to quickly check for <u>extension</u> in the attic, walls, and concealed spaces. Remember . . . Fire has taken the temper out of the garage door springs, and the door may fall (if open) at any time. Once the door is raised, it will be necessary to support it with a pike pole, ladder, etc.

**Salvage:** The remaining contents of a good garage fire usually are in such condition that salvage will be minimal. However, prompt salvage operations are necessitated in the house to reduce damage.

> *Remove/cover furnishings in the immediate area
> *Prompt ventilation in the garage and the house will reduce smoke damage
> *Floor runner
> *Salvage covers
> *Rolled plastic

A key point in any garage fire is the presence of hazardous materials. Remember to:

> *Check water run-off for pollutants
> *Decontaminate equipment
> *Decontaminate personnel

# The Alley Fire

**SCENARIO:** You roll up on the scene of a residential fire showing from the rear of the building or lot which has an alley. This scenario is typical of a garage fire; but it could be a commercial occupancy, apartment house, hotel, etc.

**STRATEGY:** The alley fire presents unique opportunities—opportunities to attack the fire as a professional and look good, as well as opportunities to make mistakes that could be catastrophic.

If the garage was well-involved with fire, your strategy would be to protect exposures, isolate and confine the fire and extinguish. Sounds simple, but it's not!

In the majority of incidents, your best chance for success is to <u>begin your attack from the street or front of the house and not the alley.</u>

By bringing hose lines from the front, fire fighters can protect the house and adjoining garages and attack the fire from the uninvolved side and push it toward the involved.

> *Hose lines positioned on either side of the garage
> *A pincer movement
> *Protect exposures and attack the fire

What if the garages exposed on the opposite side of the alley are burning? Where is the attack started? The same rules apply. The second company should lay their lines from the front of the occupancy toward the garage.

> *First, protect exposures
> *Second, attack the fire

The successful fire attack should end with the fire fighters congratulating each other on a great job in the alley. If there isn't an exposure problem on the opposite side of the alley, where is the second engine company placed? In the alley? NO!! The second engine company should come in from the same side as the first-in engine company or an adjacent street, with the objective of protecting the house, adjoining structures, and first-in personnel. Second due companies will usually:

> *Provide water supply
> *Place back-up lines in service

*Provide relief
*Assist in salvage and overhaul

What about the alley? Why didn't you attack the fire from the alley? After all, you could see the fire and you had a clear shot at it.

Experience has taught us that attacking a well-involved structure from an alley can be a strategic mistake as well as presenting unnecessary dangers to firefighters. Strategically speaking, it is best to protect exposures, stop the spread and extinguish the fire. The most valuable exposure is the house. It can be protected best by placing hose lines between the garage and the house; i.e., push the fire from the <u>uninvolved</u> back toward the <u>involved</u>. Trying to protect the house by advancing hose lines from the alley just doesn't make sense.

What happens if you attack the fire from the alley? Assuming that a supply line is laid and the apparatus is spotted in the alley:
    *How many exposures can you protect?
    *What type of hose lay would work best?

Alleys are narrow; fire apparatus is wide. Many departments use transverse 1 1/2" or 1 3/4" hose beds, oftentimes preconnected. If the transverse hose bed is used, the hose will pull out at a right angle, which causes binding and requires staffing to overcome the problem. What if we use the rear hose bed? NO!! It's facing away from the fire.

In order to advance the hose forward, a hose lay will have to be used that will place the hose to the rear and side. This way, when the hose is advanced through the narrow opening between the apparatus and the buildings, fences, etc., in the end it will not bind or snag.

What are the hazards of placing apparatus and personnel in alleys with a structure well involved?
    1) Power lines
    2) Electrocution
    3) Apparatus becomes an exposure problem
    4) Limited space creates dangerous working
        conditions

Power lines are usually run through alleys. Just about the time fire fighters have their hose lines in position to attack the well-involved structure, the flames weaken the wires; they break and fall in, on, and about fire fighters. If no one gets hurt, it's fun to watch. If this isn't enough excitement, picture the fire spreading to the power poles and having a 500-pound transformer fall. No thanks!!

What about the apparatus? Being responsible for burning the paint off the apparatus is not really a macho thing to do.

What happens if???
    *There is a delay in getting water from the
      hydrant?
    *You empty your water tank?
    *A hose line breaks?
    *Murphy's law takes charge of the fire?

The fire spreads to adjoining structures and exposures and because the apparatus is in the direct path of the fire, it becomes the most important exposure in town and the most embarrassing.

How about spotting the apparatus at the end of the alley and hand- laying attack lines down the alley?
    *Poor choice for first-in company.
    *Remember to cut off the spread.
    *The best chance of protecting exposures is
      by attacking the fire from the front street or
      uninvolved area.
    *If power lines are not a problem and there are
      access problems on the street behind the
      fire, consider back-up lines being laid down
      the alleys.

What can we expect from the garage fire itself? If you were to poll fire fighters across the country, they would probably agree that garage fires make the neatest, most spectacular fires. Don't tell Joe Citizen what they say, but they are interesting fires because they are spectacular, usually short in duration, life hazard is generally not a problem, you can handle them with one or two engine companies, and no matter how bad your strategy and tactics, they usually go out.

The experienced firefighter recognizes that the garage fire can be one of the most hazardous fires he will go to. Why?? Just about anything and everything is stored in garages. Look at your own.
    - Gasoline          -Insecticide
    - Paint             -Pesticide
    - LPG barbecue tanks    - Fertilizers, etc.
    - Substantial amounts of overhead storage

*Each garage fire is a potential HAZ-MAT problem. Caution is the name of the game. Remember:
- Adequate GPM
- Water run-off polluted with contaminates
- Personnel decontamination
- Equipment decontamination

What about the garage door? The lifting mechanism of most garage doors uses springs to gain the mechanical advantage. If the fire has burned for any length of time at all, the garage door will be in the closed position upon arrival. Remember:

*Fire has taken the temper out of the springs and the door has fallen or was already closed.

*Opening the door can be a three-act play. Garage doors are heavy, and it will usually take at least two fire fighters to raise it and at least one on a protective hose line.

*Once the door is raised, it will be necessary to support it with a pike pole, ladder, etc., because the springs have lost their temper and will not be able to help.

# Alley Fire

## Fire Problem #4-2

**DISPATCH INFORMATION**: VIDEO FOOTAGE

You have just received an alarm to respond to a garage on fire in the alley of a residential neighborhood. From the location of the address, you realize that this fire is in an older part of town. The garage is made of standard wood frame construction and is located directly on the alley at the rear of a single-family house. It is closely surrounded by adjacent wood frame structures and has additional exposures on both sides of the alley.

The time of alarm is 3:30 p.m. with a temperature of 73° F., humidity of 15%, and winds from the south at 15 M.P.H.

**ARRIVAL INFORMATION**: FIRE SLIDE

Upon arrival, you find the garage at the rear of the house fully involved on the side facing the alley. Heavy flames and smoke are extending above the garage and are threatening adjacent structures as well as the garage directly across the alley. Piles of old lumber and trash surrounding the burning garage are also on fire.

You are responding with your department's first alarm assignment and your engine company is first on the scene.

"LET'S           FIGHT           THIS           FIRE"

70

# ALLEY FIRE
## Figure 4-2

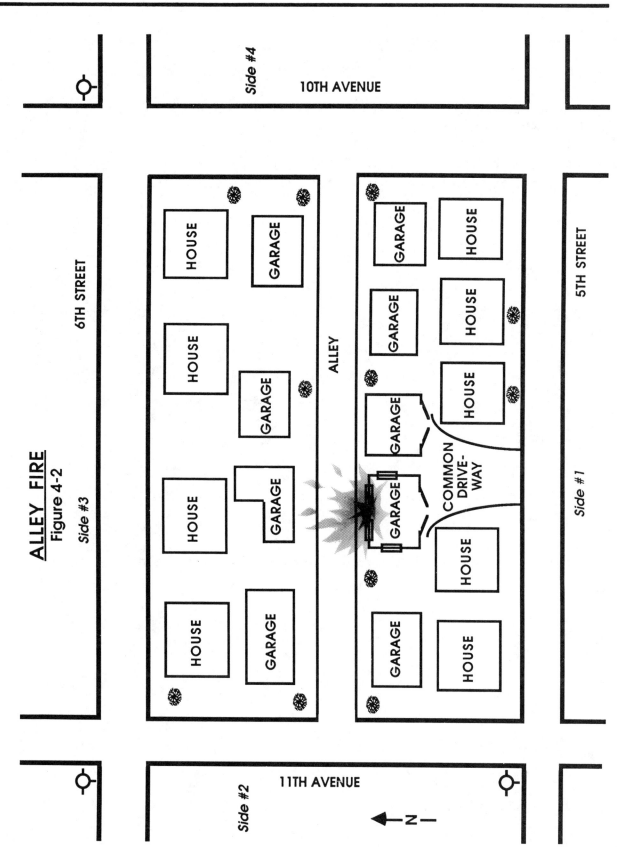

## * * STUDENT ACTIVITY * *
### Fire  Problem  #4-2

1. Carefully study the floor plan and fire photo for fire problem 4-2 and read the dispatch
   information.

2. As first officer on the scene, write a brief narrative of your arrival report:

3. Using <u>REVAS</u>, what were your incident priorities and how were they addressed?

RESCUE:

EVACUATION:

VENTILATION:

ATTACK:

SALVAGE:

4. On the floor plan draw the location of:

       1) Responding apparatus
       2) Fire attack hose lines
       3) Water supply
       4) Location and method of ventilation

5. How would you manage this incident? Draw an incident command structure that you would use on this problem.

# MODULE FIVE

## COMMERCIAL FIRE ATTACK

# VIDEO NOTES

_____

_____

_____

_____

_____

_____

_____

_____

_____

_____

_____

_____

_____

_____

_____

_____

_____

_____

_____

_____

_____

# COMMERCIAL FIRE ATTACK

In Module Five, we will review two of the most common commercial fires responded to by the American fire service: 1) the common attic, and 2) light manufacturing complex.

The small neighborhood shopping center is an excellent example of a common attic structure. Fires in this type of occupancy present very specific problems to the fireground participant. The light manufacturing or light industrial complex has become common in the United States during the past 20 years. Furniture manufacturing, machine shops, etc., which incorporate office, assembling, and warehousing are typical of this type of occupancy. Fires in a light manufacturing complex not only offer the fire fighter a variety of unique fire problems but can also have a severe impact on the economy of a community if the business is lost. Module Five will look at many of the fire problems encountered during commercial fire attack and how they can be avoided or overcome utilizing proven fireground techniques.

## The Common Attic Fire

One of the most common of the commercial fires is the common attic occupancy. What is meant by a common attic occupancy? A typical common attic occupancy has at least one wall separating occupancies that share a common attic space. Small neighborhood shopping centers are an excellent example of a common attic occupancy.

*Typical tenants include:
- 7-11 Stores
- Cleaners
- Doughnut shops
- Fast food stores
- Liquor stores
- Clothing stores

The size of the common attic space above these occupancies is controlled by local building codes. The general rule is to require attic separation walls, or draft curtains, to keep this attic space to a reasonable size so that in the event of a fire there is less chance for spread. The size of this attic space is usually figured on a formula that takes into consideration the type of construction, zoning regulations, and intended use of the occupancy. U.B.C. allows a maximum attic space of 3,000 sq.ft. before a draft curain is required.

As a general rule, these attic spaces will be as large as the law will allow. In the absence of good building regulations, attic separation walls will be left out in an effort to reduce construction cost.

Problems with common attic occupancies become particulary difficult in buildings that have been remodeled. It is not uncommon to find older buildings that have been remodeled numerous times. This presents you, the firefighter, with a number of problems when combating a common attic fire.
*Concealed spaces throughout the building
*Multiple dropped ceilings
*Layered T-Bar ceilings
*Hidden fires that are difficult to find

Common attic occupancies built prior to the late 1960s or early 1970s usually have plaster or drywall ceilings and utilize conventional construction. This type of construction provides better fire resistance than the modern lightweight truss construction that is commonly used today.

Most common attic occupancies constructed since the early 1970s utilize lightweight truss systems:
*Wooden I Beam
*Gusset plate
*Open web

Occasionally, a drywall ceiling is used with these types of trusses. However, the most common type of ceiling is the hung or suspended ceiling. Some common types are:
*T-Bar ceiling
*Celotex tiles
*Many are supported by wires attached to trusses.
*Has no fire rating

This type of ceiling creates some unique fire fighting

problems. Unlike the older conventional construction that utilizes rafters between partition walls to support the plaster or drywall as well as support the partition walls, buildings with T-Bar suspended ceilings have walls that may stop as soon as they clear the T-Bar ceiling. These are <u>partition walls</u>, also referred to as dimising walls, and their only purpose is to <u>separate occupancies</u>.

### What is a dimising wall?

Demising walls are essentially any non-weightbearing wall. They generally do not go to the roof, but sometimes they are carried to the roof and covered with drywall and used as draft curtains. Sometimes these demising walls will be constructed from floor to roof, but the drywall will generally stop just above the T-Bar ceiling. Of the dimising walls that do not go to the roof, it is common to find chicken wire or fencing material connected between the top of the wall and roof for security purposes. Some tenants require their demising walls to be covered with drywall from floor to ceiling for security purposes. Remember this wall is not a fire wall.

A long row of commercial occupancies may have several stores divided by partial height demising walls. One can see that once a fire burns through the T-Bar celotex ceiling, the fire is free to travel until it reaches a draft curtain or fire wall.

### What is a draft curtain?

It is a barrier built in an attic to stop the spread of smoke. It is not a fire wall, nor will it stop fire. Draft curtains may run from floor to ceiling or be suspended from the ceiling. The uniform building code requires draft curtains every 3,000 sq. ft. of attic space. Larger common attic buildings will generally have a fire separation or shear wall, to limit the attic space to approximately 8,000 sq. ft. In areas of the country where earthquakes are possible, this shear wall is used to stabilize the building. It is usually made of reinforced metal or wood studs covered with plywood. The plywood is then covered with 5/8" drywall on both sides, and this wall is now a firewall and has a <u>two-hour</u> rating.

### STRATEGY AND TACTICS:

How does one fight a fire in a common attic commercial building built with conventional

construction?

First let us think of:

**Rescue/Evacuation:** The rescue problem presented by a fire in such a building does not usually present special problems. Evacuation can present a problem in these occupancies, particularly if they are small shopping centers with small parking areas. It is entirely possible for a small fire to burn in a remote location and extend into the attic. There have been numerous instances where the attic area has been well-involved with fire and little or no odor of smoke in the occupancies below.

Firefighters arrive on the scene, pull the ceiling at the point of origin, discover the attic fire, and then tell shoppers to evacuate the stores. The shoppers cannot see or smell smoke, think the fire fighters are crazy or practicing again, and continue shopping until the ceiling begins to fall in.

**Ventilation:** A ventilation hole should be cut as close to the seat of the fire as can be done safely. If the fire has not spread throughout the attic yet, this hole will help to confine the fire and stop its horizontal spread.

If the fire has already burned through the roof, which is common with plywood roofs, consider using strip ventilation to help confine the fire. A common mistake made on the fireground is to believe that when the fire burns through the roof no additional ventilation is necessary.

While it has partially self-ventilated, it probably has not self-ventilated enough to stop the horizontal spread through the attic. If the initial ventilation hole that is cut or the self-ventilation holes are not adequate to stop the horizontal spread of fire, consider strip ventilation cuts that exist on either side of the first ventilation hole. This system of venting the fire, then followed by isolating it with strip ventilation cuts has proven to work quite well in stopping running attic fires. Prescribed ventilation safety considerations should be used and caution should be taken when working on plywood roofs because these types of roofs can self-ventilate very quickly during a fire. Strip ventilation requires careful coordination with the engine companies assisting below.

The strip cut by itself will not stop the fire. It may slow it down, but it will not stop it. The strip cut will slow down the horizontal spread and provide engine company personnel below with the opportunity to push the fire back toward the point of origin.

**Attack:** Where is the fire going?

Where is the area of most value?

With a long common attic occupancy and a well-involved fire in the center, how would you attack the fire?

What is your strategy?! The strategy is to cut off the fire and stop the horizontal spread.
　　　　*Downwind
　　　　*To the area of most value

If the center occupancy is well-involved, get ahead of the fire and take your lines into the adjoining occupancies:
　　　　*Pull the ceilings
　　　　*Strip ventilate
　　　　*Push the fire back into the involved area

Remember: A fire in a common attic constructed building can experience horizontal spread in both directions. Don't forget to place exposure lines to the opposite side of your attack when resources become available.

**Salvage:** A quick aggressive attack on the seat of the fire is the best way to reduce the fire loss.

Depending on available resources, salvage work should begin as soon as possible:
　　　　*Salvage covers
　　　　*Floor runners
　　　　*Plastic
　　　　*Pressurize building

A major problem involving fires in common attic occupancies is the smoke travel. When resources become available, begin to pressurize each business individually. This will greatly reduce the smoke damage that adjoining businesses experience.

80

# Common Attic

## Fire Problem #5-1

**DISPATCH INFORMATION**:  VIDEO FOOTAGE

While on routine night patrol, a local police officer discovers a fire in progress at a nearby dry cleaners store. The dry cleaners is located in a commercial strip shopping center constructed of wood frame and masonry block. The roof is made of wood truss joists with asphalt and gravel overlay.  The small shopping center is about 25 years old and was built during a period when city building codes were rarely enforced.

The time is 2:30 a.m. with a temperature of 65° F.,  and the winds are calm.

**ARRIVAL INFORMATION**:  FIRE SLIDE

Upon arrival, you see heavy smoke coming from the roof areas along the entire length of the shopping center.  Flames are visible at the ceiling level within the dry cleaners as you approach the building and look through the windows.

You are responding with your department's first alarm assignment and your engine company is first on the scene.

**"LET'S**                 **FIGHT**                 **THIS**                 **FIRE"**

# COMMON ATTIC
## Figure 5-1

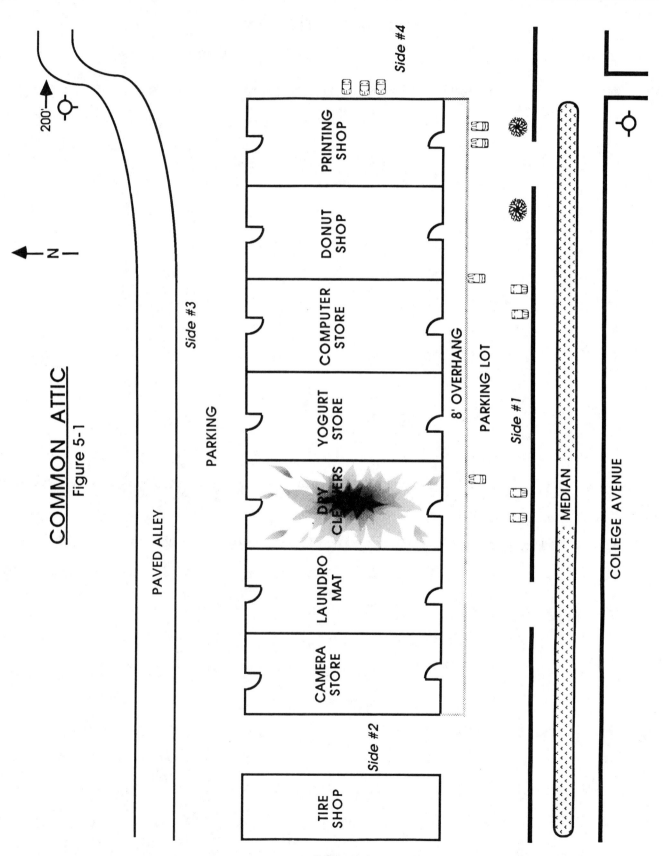

N ←

200'

PAVED ALLEY

PARKING

*Side #3*

TIRE SHOP

*Side #2*

CAMERA STORE

LAUNDRO MAT

DRY CLEANERS

YOGURT STORE

COMPUTER STORE

DONUT SHOP

PRINTING SHOP

*Side #4*

8' OVERHANG

PARKING LOT

*Side #1*

MEDIAN

COLLEGE AVENUE

83

## * * STUDENT ACTIVITY * *
### Fire Problem #5-1

1. Carefully study the floor plan and fire photo for fire problem 5-1 and read the dispatch information.

2. As first officer on the scene, write a brief narrative of your arrival report:

3. Using <u>REVAS</u>, what were your incident priorities and how were they addressed?

RESCUE:

EVACUATION:

VENTILATION:

ATTACK:

SALVAGE:

4. On the floor plan draw the location of:

     1) Responding apparatus
     2) Fire attack hose lines
     3) Water supply
     4) Location and method of ventilation

5. How would you manage this incident? Draw an incident command structure that you would use on this problem.

# The Light Manufacturing Fire

Just about every community has a light manufacturing or light industrial district, which includes:
- *Furniture manufacturing
- *Machine shop
- *Woodworking
- *Packaging
- *Laundries
- *Sweatshops

Fires in these types of occupancies can often have a severe negative impact on the economy of the community.
- *Impact on jobs
- *Impact on support businesses
- *Impact on a community's tax base

The typical light manufacturing occupancy is one or two stories. Construction features vary, but the newer buildings are usually masonry, concrete tilt-up with panelized or trussed roofs, or pre- fabricated metal buildings, sometimes referred to as Butler buildings. The occupancy will generally consist of an office area, usually at the front of the building with the rest of the building devoted to a manufacturing/storage area. If you could only save one of these areas in a fire which would you save?
- *The office area?
- *Or, the manufacturing/storage area?

If we save the office area, what are we saving?
- *Records
- *Customer lists
- *Vendor lists
- *Billing records
- *Debts/credits
- *Fire insurance policy

If we save the manufacturing/storage area, what are we saving?
- *Tools
- * Machinery
- *Product
- *Supplies
- *Inventory

All of the above items are important and represent a substantial investment, but the vast majority of the items can be replaced, usually with fire insurance. That is, of course, assuming that the fire insurance policy did not burn up with the office area. By saving the office area, we are also saving the records; and, in many cases, the business too!
- *New machinery can be purchased.
- *Specialized tools, etc.

Most importantly, the accounts receivable list is saved, so the owner can collect on bills that will not be covered by insurance. Also the list of customers is saved, so they can be notified that, "there has been a slight problem which may result in a possible delivery delay, but we are still in business!"

## STRATEGY AND TACTICS

**SCENARIO:** You come onto the scene of a one-story commercial building, 50 x 100, doing business as Widget Light Manufacturing. The building is heavily charged with smoke. There is an alley at the rear. How do we attack this fire? Let us go back to:

**Rescue/Evacuation:** In this type of occupancy, the rescue problem is usually indicated by:
- *The time of day

**86**

*Circumstances causing the fire
*Industrial accident
*Explosion, etc.
*Checking with a responsible person on the
  scene to get a head count of employees

**Ventilation:** Ventilation strategy will be to stop the horizontal spread by venting the fire vertically.
  *Use prescribed ventilation safety
    considerations
  *Vent as close to the seat of the fire as can be
    done safely
  *Special consideration and caution should be
    given to ventilation of metal frame structures,
    as early roof failure is common

If the initial ventilation hole does not stop the horizontal spread, or if the fire has self-ventilated, consider using strip ventilation as a defensive tool.
  *Strip ventilate on the safe side of separating
    walls
  *Coordinate strip ventilation with engine
    personnel below

**Attack the Fire:** Do we attack it from the front or rear?

Attacking the fire from the front of the building may be the best strategy if:
  *Protecting the office area is a prime
    consideration
  *Entry through rear alley doors is extremely
    difficult due to higher security, which would
    result in a delay in water application

What if the fire is at the front of the building? Won't an attack from the front push the fire into the rest of the building?

**Yes, and no.** This is a judgment call. Remember: Save the office area if at all possible. If you can get a good shot at the fire from the front and stop it from spreading, take it. This is a calculated risk. If you hold off your attack and take time to force entry from the rear, how far will the fire spread? The chances are good that if the fire attack is well coordinated between properly performed ventilation and well-placed hoselines, you can limit the spread of fire and extinguish it.

What size hoselines should be used for the fire attack? Remember: A minimum of 1-1/2-inch line for structure

fire fighting. For fighting fire in office areas, the smaller 1-1/2 or 1-3/4-inch hose lines are more maneuverable than larger hose lines.

A 2-1/2-inch hoseline can be used effectively for interior attacks, but you have to take into consideration the layout and obstacles that you will have to overcome as well as resources available. If you have ever tried to advance a loaded 2-1/2-inch line through a maze of office hallways, you learned that the first corner you encountered was an obstacle. It will usually require that a fire fighter stay at each corner as the loaded 2-1/2-inch progresses. The same problem will be experienced with smaller hose lines, but to a lesser degree.

If you take a 2-1/2-inch attack line in from the front to attack the manufacturing/storage area at the rear, what type of nozzle will you use — spray or straight stream? Small commercial occupancies provide the fire fighter the opportunity to utilize a variety of nozzles and related appliances.

This is a controversial subject to some fire fighters and departments. Let's do a quick review.
  *Combination nozzle:
    - More versatile
    - Adjustable stream
    -Provides more protection from
      radiated heat
    -Less nozzle reaction, more easily
      handled
  *Straight stream:
    -Better penetration
    - More nozzle reaction
    - Requires more personnel to control

The argument really boils down to versatility versus better penetration. Most experienced officers favor the modern spray nozzle because of its versatility and the protection it provides when used for an interior attack.

For large outdoor fires, straight tip nozzles are often preferred:
  *Lumber yards
  *Outside storage
  *Anything that requires extended reach

What if we have a partial burn-out of our light manufacturing building? Let's say the manufacturing area is well involved — how do we fight the fire?

Whenever fire breaks through the roof or ventilation holes, there is usually a tendency to go to elevated heavy streams and direct them at this highly visible red stuff. Is this effective? No!! But it happens all the time. General rule of thumb:

      *The elevated heavy streams go up
      *The walls go down!

Why?
It is hard to put a fire out when most of the burning contents are covered by a roof designed to keep water out of the building.

How, then, do you extinguish the fire?
If at all possible, hit it with 2-1/2-inch hand lines and/or portable monitors from below. If we cannot get access at the fire from below, then your best bet is:

      *To protect the offices, if possible
      *To protect adjacent exposures
      *Utilize elevated heavy streams
      *Produce good news footage

A word of caution!! The Incident Commander should notify all officers on the fireground that heavy streams will be placed into operation as soon as he can verify that all personnel are out of the building. This represents a switch from an offensive to a defensive attack. <u>Make sure you account for all your personnel!</u>

**Salvage:** This can be critical in light manufacturing types of occupancy and should receive a high priority. The use of computer-related equipment in many manufacturing processes creates a very difficult salvage operation for fire personnel. Utilize your resources to the best advantage. Save the records and files that can't be replaced first; then, concentrate on the most valuable equipment items.

      *Remove and cover equipment as soon as
       possible
      *Salvage covers
      *Floor runners
      *Plastic
      *Pressurize the building to reduce smoke
       damage

# Light Manufacturing

## Fire Problem #5-2

**DISPATCH INFORMATION**: VIDEO FOOTAGE

You have just received an alarm to respond to a reported structure fire in a light manufacturing business. From your pre-fire plan book, you remember that this business manufactures electronic test equipment for the B-1 Bomber. The building is constructed of pre-cast concrete panels and masonry block construction throughout. The roof is constructed with steel bar joist trusses, plywood roof decking, and overlayed with asphalt and gravel. The manufacturing firm employs about 35 workers and maintains tight security around the property at all times.

The time of alarm is 1:20 p.m. with a temperature of 81° F. and the winds are calm.

**ARRIVAL INFORMATION**: FIRE SLIDE

Upon arrival you see light smoke coming from the roof of the warehouse/workshop area. Heavy black smoke is showing from the roof vents located near the center of the building. You are met by a hysterical owner who states that there was an explosion in the paint room. Two employees have been injured and they are unaccounted for.

You are responding with your department's first alarm assignment and your engine company is first on the scene.

**"LET'S            FIGHT            THIS            FIRE"**

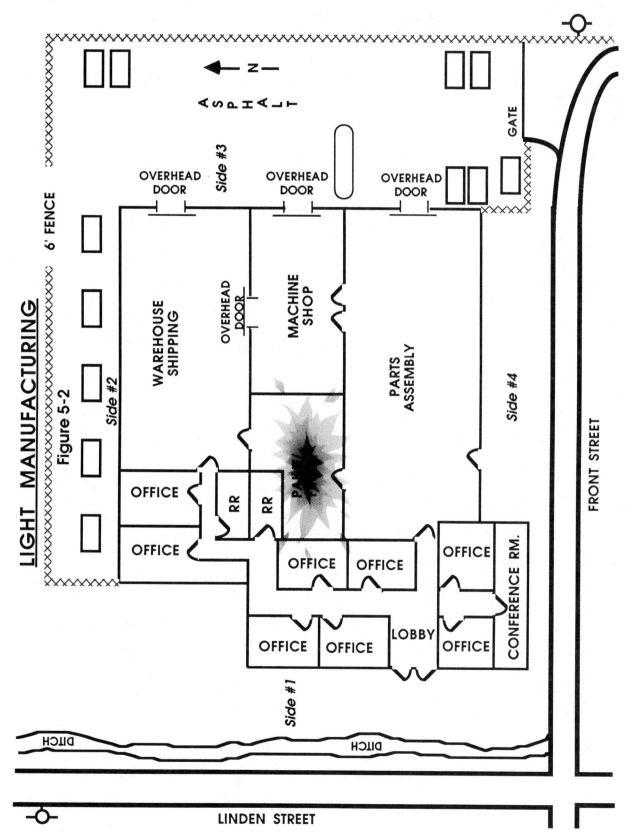

LIGHT MANUFACTURING

Figure 5-2

6' FENCE

Side #2

Side #1

Side #3

Side #4

N

ASPHALT

GATE

OVERHEAD DOOR

OVERHEAD DOOR

OVERHEAD DOOR

OVERHEAD DOOR

WAREHOUSE SHIPPING

MACHINE SHOP

PARTS ASSEMBLY

OFFICE

OFFICE

RR

RR

OFFICE

OFFICE

OFFICE

OFFICE

LOBBY

OFFICE

OFFICE

CONFERENCE RM.

DITCH

DITCH

FRONT STREET

LINDEN STREET

91

## * * STUDENT ACTIVITY * *
### Fire Problem #5-2

1. Carefully study the floor plan and fire photo for fire problem 5-2 and read the dispatch information.

2. As first officer on the scene, write a brief narrative of your arrival report:

3. Using <u>REVAS</u>, what were your incident priorities and how were they addressed?

RESCUE:

EVACUATION:

92

VENTILATION:

ATTACK:

SALVAGE:

4. On the floor plan draw the location of:

      1) Responding apparatus
      2) Fire attack hose lines
      3) Water supply
      4) Location and method of ventilation

5. How would you manage this incident? Draw an incident command structure that you would use on this problem.

# MODULE SIX

## ABOVE-GROUND FIRE ATTACK

# VIDEO NOTES

_____

_____

_____

_____

_____

_____

_____

_____

_____

_____

_____

_____

_____

_____

_____

_____

_____

_____

_____

_____

_____

# ABOVE-GROUND FIRE ATTACK

Module Six will cover one of the toughest fires combatted by the American fire service, the above-ground fire. Above-ground firefighting can be separated into two main categories: 1) center hallway, and 2) center core.

Center hallway occupancies are usually multiple-story buildings that utilize a central corridor to access individual sleeping rooms or apartments.

Center core constructed buildings are also multiple-story buildings that utilize a central core area for elevators, stairways, and utility shafts. A three-story office complex, hermetically sealed with offices located to the outside wall of the building, is a good example.

Module Six will explore the multitude of fire problems which will be encountered when combatting fires in these types of occupancies. You will draw from the experience of your instructors to learn proven fire attack methods, which will help you avoid and over come many of the difficulties you face when responding to a low-rise fire.

## The Center Hallway Occupancy

One of the toughest fires to fight is the center hallway occupancy. What is it? It is a building, usually several floors in height, with a central corridor or hallway that is used for access to the rooms. This type of construction has been used for hundreds of years and is still cost effective today. It is used in apartment houses, hotels, and office buildings. The main fire problem is in apartment houses and hotels, due mainly to the higher frequency of fires coupled with the fact that many of the older buildings end up as slum tenements.

Why is this type of fire so difficult to fight?
  *Normally high life hazard
  *Marginal building conditions often exist
  *Immediate smoke problems due to common
   hallway
  *Increased set-up time for attacking the fire

First, let us discuss the burning characteristics of this type of building and some of the more common problems they can present.
  * A small one-room fire in a center hallway
   building can cause serious problems to the
   occupants as soon as the smoke enters the
   common hallway.
  * The smoke in the hallway affects the people
   attempting to evacuate the building,
   sometimes causing panic.
  * The occupants are forced to evacuate
   through a common hallway filled with smoke.
  * If the fire is unchecked, it will grow in size until
   it spreads into the hallway. Eventually, the
   hallway becomes a raging inferno spreading
   flames into the adjoining occupancies.
  * If the fire doors are open in the hallways, we
   now have a problem with mushrooming. In
   other words, the hot air and gases rise up the
   stair shafts until they hit the top floor. If the fire
   doors are open, the smoke will fill that floor and
   other floors with smoke as it "mushrooms"
   down. We now have a very serious fire
   problem, both for the occupants and the fire
   fighters.
  * A word about fire doors . . . there are all types
   of fire doors equipped with automatic closing
   devices. Unfortunately, particularly in older
   buildings with poor air circulation and security
   problems, these doors are often wedged
   open and are useless as fire stops during a
   fire.

A general rule of thumb used by experienced fire fighters concerning hallway fire doors is:
  *They are supposed to be closed
  *They are probably jammed open
  *They will change position during the course
   of the fire

We now have a very serious fire problem, both for the occupants and the fire fighters. The occupants' main problem is that their main means of escape, the center hallway, is cut off by smoke, heat, and fire. This leaves the occupants with three ways to survive.
  *Jump from the structure
  *External ladder rescue

*Keep the corridor door closed, and pray it doesn't burn through before fire fighters can extinguish the fire.

None of these choices sound very good, but this scenario is played out on a routine basis across the country.

What type of problems will the firefighter encounter?
*With flames in the central hallway and adjoining occupancies, fire fighters will essentially be attacking a fire in a tunnel.

The name of the game in attacking the fire will be multiple hand lines carefully coordinated:
1-1/2-inch hose
1-3/4-inch hose
2-1/2-inch hose

It will take a minimum of two lines to safely attack this fire.
*One to hold the hallway
*One to extinguish individual occupancies that are involved in fire

This makes sense and sounds simple, but the operation requires a great deal of coordination, particularly when extending lines in a hot smoke-filled hallway with communication limited, at best.
*First, shut one line down to extend it
*Then, keep the second line flowing to control heat in hallway and protect personnel

**SCENARIO I:** How do we fight a one-room fire in a center hallway occupancy where the fire has not entered into the hallway?

**STRATEGY AND TACTICS**
First let us think of

**Rescue:**
*With a small fire, the rescue problem is not as severe
*Possibility of panic could cause problems

**Evacuate:**
*Usually not a serious problem
*Have residents leave immediate area by separate stairway not being used by fire fighters

**Ventilate:**
*Ventilation team makes assessment starting at top of building

*Open penthouse door
*Check fire doors on way down
*Reassure occupants
*Pressurize building at ground floor with smoke ejectors
*If it is not possible to pressurize at ground floor, pressurize at opposite ends of the hallway
*In either case, the smoke will be confined to immediate fire area and will be evacuated through the apartment windows

**Attack:**

*Apparatus placement can be critical
*Buildings of five or less stories: spot Engine Company closest to the building and Truck Company toward the middle of the street for aerial access
*Aerial to roof
*Smoke showing from second or third floor: still place aerial to roof for use of ventilation team
*Buildings over five stories: spot the aerial inside to gain reach and Engine Company outside
*Investigation team consisting of an officer and two fire fighters enters building from ground floor
*Equipped with:
  -Protective clothing
  -Self-contained breathing apparatus
  -Forcible entry tool
  -1-1/2" or 1-3/4" hose pack
  -Fire extinguisher
  -Drop bags for all personnel
  -Portable radio
*As the fire investigation team moves from floor to floor, they notify the Incident Commander of conditions; i.e.,
  - "First floor, ok"
  - "Second floor, light smoke"
  - "Third floor, one-room fire. We are going to bring an attack line in with a

drop bag from the front of the building."
*Drop bag versus ground ladders or stairway can provide a quick means of getting hose lines to the fire floor
*Fire on first or second floor: direct attack using stairwells, if necessary
*Second floor through fifth floor: drop bag system is fastest and most efficient
*Interior wet standpipe systems:
  -- Good Luck!
  -- Not reliable
  -- Last resort
*Keep door closed to the apartment until the hose line is in position and charged
*Radio ventilation team to pressurize building
*Open door and extinguish fire

**Salvage:**

*Try to use as little water as possible in attacking fire
*Pressurize building with smoke ejectors to reduce smoke damage
*Assign personnel to check for water below the fire
*Place salvage cover on floor and overhaul as much debris as possible in room rather than carrying smoking debris through building to overhaul outside

**SCENARIO II:** How do we fight a fire in a center-hallway occupancy where the fire has spread into the hallway and adjoining occupancies? Smoke has spread throughout the building and mushrooming is a factor.

This fire is relatively simple, right?

**Wrong** -- this fire is going to be tough! And, if you handle it wrong, it could result in:
  *Civilian injuries and/or life loss
  *Burning the building down
  *Burning adjoining buildings down
  *Fire fighter injuries and/or life loss

99

## STRATEGY AND TACTICS

First, let us think of Chief Revas:

**Rescue/Evacuation:**   The time of day, weekday or weekend, will give a good indication of the severity of the rescue problem:
> *Nighttime: Apartment house--severe life hazard. Office building--slight life hazard
> *Daytime: Apartment house--slight life hazard. Office building--severe life hazard

Regardless of the above, rescue will have to be a prime consideration.
> *Vacant/abandoned building filled with indigents
> *With fire and/or smoke in the hallways, the exit path is cut off for the occupants

It is not uncommon to have people waiting for rescue at windows and/or fire escapes.

Experience has shown us that <u>for every person at the window, you have two or three down in the hallway.</u>

The key to this type of fire is
> <u>KEEP THE HALLS TENABLE!!</u>

Do we commit our first-in resources to rescue/evacuation, or do we attack the fire?   By committing our resources to rescue/evacuation:
> *The fire grows in intensity

*More smoke/heat is generated making the hallways untenable
*You may lose more people because of these decisions

By committing our resources to the fire attack, we:
> *Reduce the volume of fire
> *Reduce smoke and heat in hallways
> *You may lose more people because of these decisions

Sometimes the facts of life are not pleasant.  The decision on how we fight this fire is a judgment call and should be based on:
> *The best available information
> *Fireground experience/training
> *Available resources, etc.
> *GOOD LUCK!

### Ventilation:
<u>Remember</u>: Keep the hallways tenable.

*If at all possible, relieve the smoke and heat by ventilating at the top of the building.
> - Commit ventilation teams to the roof
> - Check penthouse for smoke and open door
> - Check light wells over stair shafts for smoke and then open up
> - <u>If fire conditions dictate, make center hallway cut</u>
> - Pressurize building with blowers as soon as conditions allow

*If the fire is on the top floor or fire has spread through pipe alleys/hoses:
> - Vent roof
> - Strip ventilation

### Attack:
Your strategy should be to push the fire from the uninvolved area back into the involved, if possible.  In either case, the fire will be fought in the hallway working from one end to the other.

Consider: The hallway will be hot!!
> - Very hot!
> - Like a fire in a tunnel or the hold of a ship
> - A well-involved room fire that has extended into the hallway will produce one of the most intense, dangerous fires you will ever combat

Multiple handlines will be required, specifically:

**100**

- 1-1/2" or 1-3/4" lines
- Side-by-side attack
- One line holds the hallway while the other extinguishes rooms

Bring handlines into position:
- Up stair shaft from floor below
- Through windows in uninvolved area of fire floor. Plan ahead for relief of attack personnel.
- Extreme heat will cause exhaustion

If the fire is on the top floor:
- Check for running attic fire
- Pull ceilings
- Pull ceilings and make a big hole
- Coordinate attack on top floor with ventilation team
- Strip ventilation to cut it off

## Salvage:

The Incident Commander will have his hands full handling the attack portion of this fire.

Help is as close as your Incident Command System Tool Box.

Create a Salvage Division on the floor below the fire and delegate this responsibility.
- Salvage covers
- Plastic
- Sawdust
- Mops, brooms
- Water chutes
- Hard work

## TRAINING EXERCISE

A good company training exercise that teaches fire fighters the coordination needed to make an effective attack on common hallway occupancies is illustrated In Figures 1 and 2. An advantage to this training exercise is the limited equipment needed to conduct the drill.

**Performance Objective:** Place two lines in-service into the hallway.

Figure 1)Shut one line down to extend it by the addition of another length of hose, while the second hose line holds the hallway.

Figure 2) Coordinate controlling the heat in the hallway, while attacking each room individually.

**Equipment Needed:** To simulate a center hallway multi-unit occupancy fire, find an open space such as a parking lot. Set up athletic weights or bricks to simulate doorways in the hallway. Place a traffic cone at the rear of each room to simulate fire location.

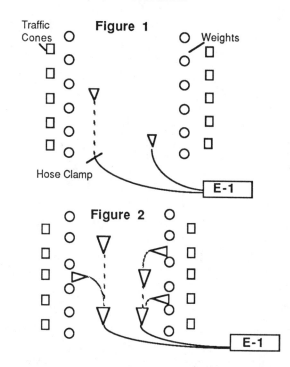

Clamp one hose line and add an additional section of hose. Coordinate a two-line attack. As line one holds the hallway, the second hose line attacks the room fire by knocking down the traffic cones. Continue down the "hallway," alternating protection and fire attack between the two lines. This exercise will clearly demonstrate the difficulty of advancing and coordinating hose lines in center hallway occupancies, especially when attack crews don't have sufficient hose to make the attack.

101

# Center Hallway

## Fire Problem #6-1

**DISPATCH INFORMATION**: VIDEO FOOTAGE

You have been dispatched to a reported structure fire in an old, four-story apartment house. This building is a four-story, center hallway structure for low-income families. The building has solid brick exterior walls with wood frame interior construction. The roof is also constructed of wood with poured tar overlayment.

The time of alarm is 3:15 p.m. with a temperature of 70° F. and the winds are calm.

**ARRIVAL INFORMATION**: FIRE SLIDE

Upon arrival, you discover heavy smoke coming from the third floor of the apartment house. Flames are showing from the third floor on the south side of the building. In addition, fire is lapping at the fourth floor. A police officer has stated to you that he tried to search the third floor but encountered too much smoke.

You are responding with your department's first alarm assignment and your engine company is first on the scene.

"LET'S                    FIGHT                    THIS                    FIRE"

104

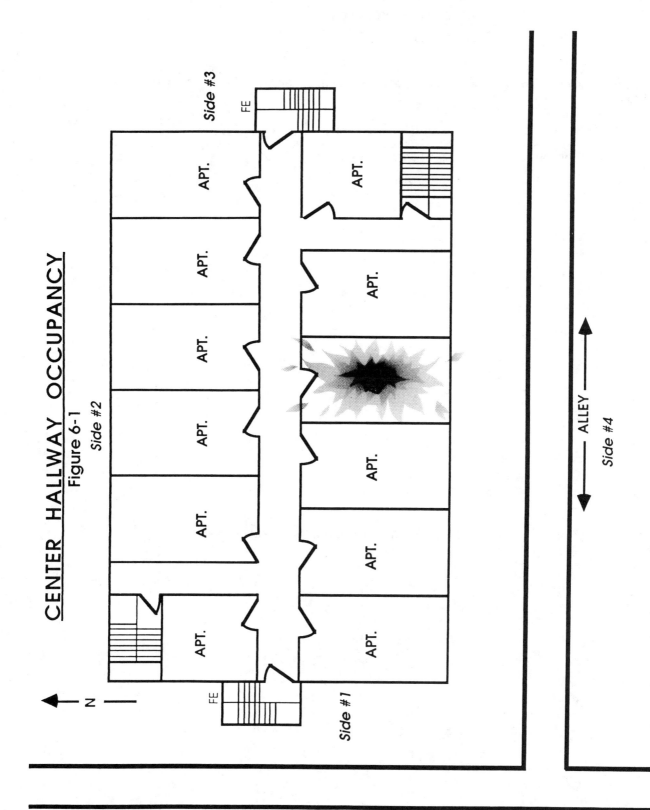

CENTER HALLWAY OCCUPANCY
Figure 6-1
Side #2

Side #3

Side #1

N

FE

FE

APT.

APT.

APT.

APT.

APT.

APT.

APT.

APT.

APT.

APT.

APT.

ALLEY

Side #4

LINCOLN AVENUE

105

# * * STUDENT ACTIVITY * *
## Fire Problem #6-1

1. Carefully study the floor plan and fire photo for fire problem 6-1 and read the dispatch information.

2. As first officer on the scene, write a brief narrative of your arrival report:

3. Using <u>REVAS</u>, what were your incident priorities and how were they addressed?

RESCUE:

EVACUATION:

**106**

VENTILATION:


ATTACK:


SALVAGE:


4. On the floor plan draw the location of:

      1) Responding apparatus
      2) Fire attack hose lines
      3) Water supply
      4) Location and method of ventilation


5. How would you manage this incident? Draw an incident command structure that you
   would use on this problem.

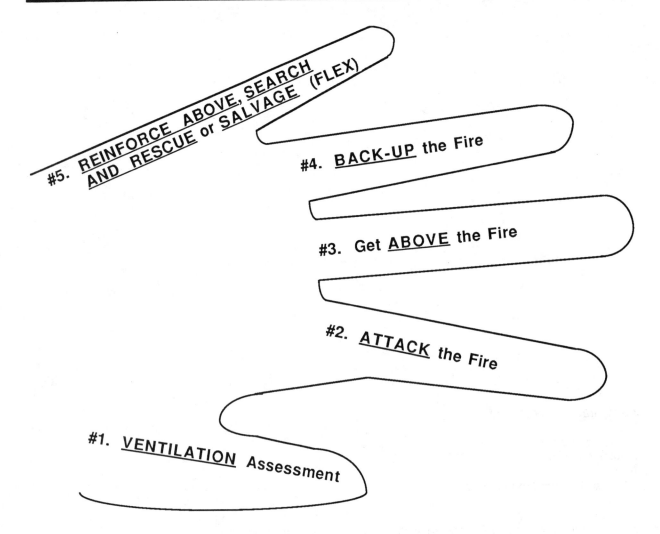

#5. REINFORCE ABOVE, SEARCH AND RESCUE or SALVAGE (FLEX)

#4. BACK-UP the Fire

#3. Get ABOVE the Fire

#2. ATTACK the Fire

#1. VENTILATION Assessment

# ABOVE-GROUND FIREFIGHTING STRATEGY

# The Center Core Occupancy

Some fire departments consider any building that cannot be reached with fire department ladders as a high-rise. Most building codes agree that a high-rise building is any structure over 75 feet tall. Buildings constructed according to high-rise standards include a whole host of built-in fire protection features that make our job easier and safer, i.e.,

*Fire control rooms
*Elevator smoke enclosures
*Sprinklers
*Combination Standpipe Systems
*Pull station fire alarm systems
*Internal communication systems
*Emergency power

These fire protection features cost money, and it is not uncommon for developers to build "low-rise" buildings to save these costs as well as comply with other density or height requirements. These 74-feet "low-rise" buildings are usually constructed in areas immediately adjacent to or mixed in with high-rise corridors.

Fire fighters must be alert to these buildings as they are usually constructed the same as high-rise buildings and look identical

*Center core construction
*Curtain-wall side coverings
*Lots of glass
*Hermetically sealed (office buildings)

What is the main difference then between the "high-rise" and "low- rise" building?
The "low-rise" building is not required to have built-in fire protection features such as:

*Fire control room
*Elevator smoke enclosures
*Sprinklers
*Combination Standpipe Systems
*Pull station fire alarm systems, unless it is a habitational occupancy
*Internal Communication System

## APPLYING THE IC SYSTEM

This type of fire is the classic example of the "either-or" fire. Either we treat it as a high-rise building, or we don't. We can fight it either way. As a result of this "either-or" situation, the fire fighting problem that usually occurs in this type of occupancy is confusion.

Confusion caused by assuming the building has built-in high-rise fire protection features, when it doesn't. Confusion caused by trying to control the smoke in the hermetically sealed office buildings. Confusion caused by using high-rise fire fighting procedures that may make the fire more complex than it is. This is where the use of the Incident Command System can reduce the confusion this type of fire will create.

As IC, do you really need:
*Lobby control?
*Resource?
*Stairwell support?
*Resource?
*Divisions?
*Groups?

Can the building be laddered from the exterior? Let's take a brief look at each of these areas in relation to a fire attack in a low-rise center core constructed building.

**Lobby Control:** Most low-rise buildings are built using construction similar to high-rise buildings. Central core construction

*Elevators and stairshafts are grouped in the center of the building with an aisle surrounding the core which allows all offices to have window access

Do we establish a lobby control?
Yes!! if we need it; and chances are we will.
*Control elevators
*Control egress and ingress to stairshafts
*Control evacuation from building

**Resource:** Will you need a resource area two floors below the fire the same way you would in a high-rise building? You might! This will depend on
*Height of the building
*Location of the fire
*Size of the fire
*Materials involved

109

Do you really need a resource area inside the building if it's six stories high and the fire is on the third floor? How about using the street?

**Staging:** This could very well be combined with staging at street level in a low-rise building fire. We definitely need a central point for incoming units to respond to in order to maintain control and avoid "free-lancing" by responding companies.

**Stairwell Support:** A stairwell support could very well be needed in the low-rise fire because of the possible lack of built-in fire protection features.
>    *Augment Standpipe System by laying supply lines in stairwell
>    *Advance fire fighting equipment
>    *Pressurize stairshafts to control smoke

**Exterior Ladders:** Remember the potential importance of fire department ladders on the exterior to attack the fire. You are dealing with buildings less than 75 feet high; and, if they are close enough to the street, you have a chance to use 100-foot aerial ladders to gain direct access to the fire floor
>    *Ladder the fire several windows from the fire
>    *Take attack lines into the uninvolved office or room and attack the fire from the hallway pushing it back into the involved area

To be a successful scene manager, you will need to address many of these problems when combatting low-rise fires. As the Incident Commander, remember the IC tool box. Use only what you need to have an effective fireground operation.

**SCENARIO:** Six-story modern, hermetically sealed, office building with fire on the fourth floor. A prior knowledge of this building through a progressive pre-fire planning program will be of great help.

## STRATEGY AND TACTICS

First, let's simplify and prioritize this fire using

**Rescue/Evacuation:** The time of day will dictate the severity of the problem
>    *Daytime: Severe
>    *Nighttime: Not so severe

Gain control of the elevators

If needed, the Incident Commander should assign a Rescue/Evacuation Division
>    *Above the fire
>    *Designate one stairway for evacuation
>    *The other stairway for ventilation

110

*Consider creating refuge areas on upper floors
*Communication between Incident Commander, Ventilation Group, and Rescue/Evacuation Division is critical

**Ventilation:**   The ventilation problem on this type of building can become complicated:
*Business buildings are hermetically sealed
*Rely totally on heating, ventilation, air condition (HVAC) for air movement
*Windows are nonopenable

HVAC systems are generally designed not to circulate smoke throughout the building.  Many are designed to remove smoke.
*Don't count on it!!
*These systems have a poor track record at actual fires
*Usually everything goes wrong, and they actually circulate smoke

The safest procedure with hermetically sealed buildings is to shut down the HVAC system, make a ventilation assessment, and then bring it back on line if you determine it will help.  A ventilation assessment will have to be made first, then:
*Designate ventilation group
*Start at top of building and work down
*Keep the Incident Commander informed by radio, i.e.,
-"Stairshaft to penthouse is clear."
-"Light smoke on sixth floor."
-"Heavy smoke on fifth floor."

Basically, there are two ways to ventilate this type of building,
1)  Break windows and cross ventilate
2)  Ventilate through stairshaft that goes through the roof

Cross ventilation
*Pressurize building's stairshafts at ground floor
*Control fire doors in stairshafts
*Break windows

Stairshaft ventilation
*Same basic procedure as cross ventilating with exception of the location of smoke exiting the building

*Open penthouse door
*Control fire doors in stairshafts
*Pressurize building stairshafts at ground floor

A few words about breaking windows:
*Try to break the tempered glass windows designated for fire department
*If they are in the wrong place, or you cannot get to them, break the windows which will solve your problem
*When breaking plate glass, try and pull the glass inside the building
*Protect people below
Ventilation group should be equipped with portable radio to keep the Incident Commander informed of status of ventilation.

**Attack the Fire:**   If the building can be reached with aerial ladders, you have two choices
1)  Attack the fire from interior stairshafts
2)  Attack the fire from the exterior by entering the building by aerial or ground ladders next to the fire and pushing it back into the involved area.

Which way would you choose?

Both systems will work, but the odds of a successful attack are better if you take it from the inside stairshafts
*Start attack from safe refuge
*Standpipes are available
*Push fire from uninvolved back into involved

If we pull up on the scene and there is nothing showing, what does the first-in company do?
*Company officer and two fire fighters start for the fire floor
*Use stairs
*Elevators are dangerous
*Equipment should include:
- Hose pack
- Forcible entry tool
- Drop bags
- SCBA
- Water extinguisher (nothing showing)
- Extra hose pack (fire showing)
- Portable radio
*Keep Incident Commander informed of location and conditions via radio:
- "First floor, okay"

-"Second floor, light smoke"
- "Third floor, moderate smoke"
- "Fourth floor, one suite well-involved; we are attacking fire from south stairwell"

*First — in truck company or designated truck functions (nothing showing) should:
-Using either aerial ladder or stairs, send ventilation team to the top of the building
-Open penthouse door
-Ventilation assessment
-Work down
Keep Incident Commander informed by radio

What about the other companies responding as part of the first alarm assignment? If, and when, do we set up lobby control? This is where pre-fire planning will pay off. These buildings will vary considerably as to their built-in fire protection features. If the decision is made to establish lobby control, it should be done early in the fire.

*Second company on scene

If the second company is a truck, and the decision is made to establish lobby, the truck may take the job depending on your overall resources. In any case, ventilation assessment will have to be an assigned duty in fires of this type.

The remaining companies should hold back from the scene, staged approximately one block from the incident, until the investigation team determines the extent of the fire problem. "Free- lancing" is one of the quickest ways to screw up a fire. If the remaining assignment reports on-scene to the Incident Commander, he can then place them according to his plan. We discover we have a working fire on the fourth floor. Where is the first attack made on the fire?
*Direct attack on the fire
*The odds are in your favor

Why? What if the fire is lapping to the upper floors?
*Attack the main body of the fire and reduce the source that is causing the fire to spread

The second fire attack should be made above the fire
*Stop vertical spread

The third fire attack company
*Backup initial attack on main fire floor

There are several choices for obtaining your water to attack the fire
1) Interior wet standpipes
*If the system is serviceable and in good shape, this system should be almost adequate for one attack line
2) Dry standpipes
*Good for multiple attack lines
*Takes time to charge system
3) Advance attack lines up stairshafts
*It will work
*Labor intensive operation
*You need many fire fighters on the scene
4) Break a window and use a drop bag to bring attack lines in on fire floor
*Very fast operation
*Requires very little staffing
*Costs building owner one window
*Protect people below
If you have extensive fire and central core construction, how do you attack the fire? The standpipe outlets will be inside the stairshaft
*This is where we will start the attack
*Hopefully, from the uninvolved side back into the involved side

What about opposing hose streams? This can be a worst-case scenario, but is there ever a time when we may have to do it? Yes, center core construction may require hoselines to come from two directions in order to prevent the fire from circling around the central core. Firefighters must understand what they are doing and, if at all possible, try to push the fire against an outside wall.

**Salvage:** Computers and record storage are the high ticket items in business buildings. Try and stay ahead of the game. There will definitely be a salvage problem below the fire. Commit companies to this assignment as early as possible. Once the lower floors are protected, don't overlook covering the computers and office equipment on the upper floors to protect them from smoke.
*Water chutes
*Pressurize building
*Salvage covers
*Plastic

# Center Core

## Fire Problem #6-2

**DISPATCH INFORMATION**: VIDEO FOOTAGE

You have just received an alarm to respond to a fire in progress at a three-story office building. The building is constructed as a type 1 non-combustible building made with brick and steel. The roof is light-weight concrete utilizing steel bar joists.

The time of alarm is 11:30 p.m. with a temperature of 68° F., and the winds are calm.

**ARRIVAL INFORMATION**: FIRE SLIDE

Upon arrival you see flames and smoke coming from the front of the building on the second floor. Building maintenance personnel meet you at the door and state that there is heavy smoke on the second floor. They further relate to you that several people routinely work all night in the computer centers located on the third floor.

You are responding with your department's first alarm assignment and your engine company is first on the scene.

**"LET'S            FIGHT            THIS            FIRE"**

# CENTER CORE FIRE

### Figure 6-2

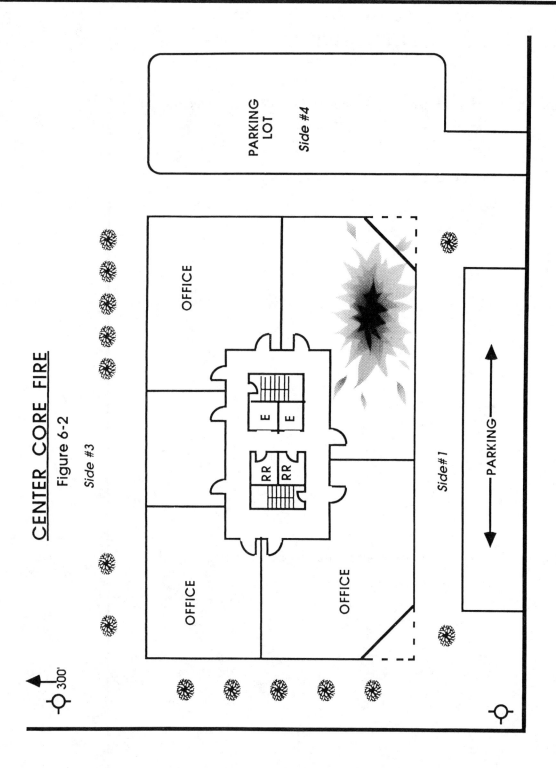

OFFICE

OFFICE

OFFICE

PARKING LOT

Side #4

Side #3

Side #1

Side #2

PARKING

23RD AVENUE

MAPLE STREET

E

E

RR

RR

N

300'

## * * STUDENT ACTIVITY * *
### Fire Problem #6-2

1.  Carefully study the floor plan and fire photo for fire problem 6-2 and read the dispatch information.

2.  As first officer on the scene, write a brief narrative of your arrival report:

3. Using <u>REVAS</u>, what were your incident priorities and how were they addressed?

RESCUE:

EVACUATION:

VENTILATION:

ATTACK:

SALVAGE:

4. On the floor plan draw the location of:

   1) Responding apparatus
   2) Fire attack hose lines
   3) Water supply
   4) Location and method of ventilation

5. How would you manage this incident?  Draw an incident command structure that you would use on this problem.